111

Morning

MEDITATIONS

111

Morning

MEDITATIONS
Create Your Day with Intention

with **Sunny Dawn Johnston**
and Contributors from Across the Globe

SDJ Productions LLC
4640 W. Redfield Road
Glendale, AZ 85306
sdjproductions.net

Because of the dynamic nature of the Internet, any web addresses or links contained in this book may have changed since publication and may no longer be valid. The original meditations and views expressed in this work are solely those of the authors.

The authors of this book do not dispense medical advice or prescribe the use of any technique as a form of treatment for physical, emotional, or medical problems without the advice of a physician, either directly or indirectly. The intent of the authors is only to offer information of a general nature to help you in your quest for emotional and spiritual well-being. In the event you use any of the information in this book for yourself, which is your constitutional right, the authors and the publisher assume no responsibility for your actions.

ISBN-13: 978-0-9961389-6-3
Library of Congress Control Number: 2017916521

Cover Design by Kris Voelker Designs
Compiled by Deb McGowan
Formatted by Shanda Trofe

Available at Amazon.com and other retailers.
Printed in the United States of America.

Dedication

This book is dedicated to the desire within ... and to those with the desire to create an intentional life by living in the present moment.
– Sunny Dawn Johnston

"I'm simply saying that there is a way to be sane. I'm saying that you can get rid of all this insanity created by the past in you. Just by being a simple witness of your thought processes.

It is simply sitting silently, witnessing the thoughts passing before you. Just witnessing, not interfering not even judging, because the moment you judge you have lost the pure witness. The moment you say "this is good, this is bad," you have already jumped onto the thought process.

It takes a little time to create a gap between the witness and the mind. Once the gap is there, you are in for a great surprise, that you are not the mind, that you are the witness, a watcher.

And this process of watching is the very alchemy of real religion. Because as you become more and more deeply rooted in witnessing, thoughts start disappearing. You are, but the mind is utterly empty.

That's the moment of enlightenment. That is the moment that you become for the first time an unconditioned, sane, really free human being."
– Osho

Contents

Introduction

"*If every 8-year-old is taught meditation, we will eliminate violence from the world within one generation.*"
–Dalai Lama

I f you are reading this book, you are probably not 8 years old, but I truly believe the statement above is true. Whether you are 8 or 48, meditation can bring you peace … and in doing so, bring world peace, one person at a time. If you have picked up this book, you are likely older than eight and looking for something within you: a new way to connect, quiet your mind and/or simply clear your head. In today's rapidly changing world, we face unique social and emotional challenges. People are experiencing greater pressures and feel more stress and anxiety than ever before.

When I heard the Dalai Lama's quote several years ago, it got me to thinking. What if we began our day with a few minutes of intention, quiet and stillness? What if we started our day intentionally instead of reactively? What if we took our power back from the stress and the worry, and directed it towards our wants and desires? What if daily morning meditation helped us become more proactive and less reactive? What might happen within us and how might that change our little corner of the world?

The goal of this book is to offer an answer to those questions. *111 Morning Meditations: Create Your Day with Intention* was created because **I LOVE Meditation.**

"Don't just medicate—meditate"
–SDJ

But it wasn't always that way. I hated it at first. It seemed hard. It was frustrating. Basically, I just didn't get the point. Mainly because everyone told me a different way to do it ... and I couldn't figure out what the right way was. Once I discovered there is no "right way", that all I needed to do was be in the moment and be present ... **I LOVED meditation.** Once I was given permission to just be present, to focus my attention on a particular set of words or affirmations or nothing at all—whatever way I desired in the moment—meditation became a powerful connection for me.

"Meditation is painful in the beginning but it bestows immortal Bliss and supreme Joy in the end."
–Swami Sivananda

I learned for myself that meditation really is about taking the time EVERY DAY to acknowledge that I am Spirit in body. When I take the time to intentionally create my day, to connect, plug in, open up to the energy or the guidance ... I feel the presence of Source (the God of your understanding) within me and my angels, guides and deceased loved ones around me. For me, it is an acknowledgement of who I truly am. I am not my head and this physical body. I am not my fears or worries. I am Spirit in this physical body. I am love and light and peace and joy.

Many of the over 80 contributors of this book are daily meditators. They have learned, through their own life experience, how important it is to be centered, grounded and present. Sharing short guided meditations, contemplations and uplifting messages is their way of bringing peace to a world that is struggling to find its harmony. Each of these amazing authors have chosen to be a light by sharing a mediation that touches their soul. That is the wonderful thing about this book ... there are a variety of unique styles of meditation, all wonderful, different and perfect in their own way. With that in mind, we have chosen to allow the authors their own creative license, acknowledging that the diversity of their writing style, often more poetic in nature, is equal to the diversity of meditation styles. Please enjoy each and every morning meditation, knowing that it comes from the heart of someone that desires to share, expand and support your meditative journey.

What is Meditation?

Meditation is a technique that is often used to focus energy, gain clarity or receive guidance. There are various forms of meditation and each person connects with meditation in a different way. **There is no RIGHT way.** Some focus on the breath, others on a reading, passage, message or affirmation, others on a vision; all to attain stillness. For when we are still, we are present; and when we are present, the fears and worries and stress drift away, leaving us with trust and hope and presence in the greatest ways possible.

"The purpose of meditation is to make our mind calm and peaceful. If our mind is peaceful, we will be free from worries and mental discomfort, and so we will experience true happiness. But if our mind is not peaceful, we will find it very difficult to be happy, even if we are living in the very best conditions."
–Kelsang Gyatso

How Do I Meditate?

There are many ways to meditate, and remember, there is NO ONE WAY to meditate. The intention of this book is to offer you a message to contemplate, feel into, follow or sit with each day for 111 days. Why 111 days? When you see a sequence of 1s show up, it is a great sign of a new opportunity. It means that a "doorway" has opened in which your intentions and goals will manifest extremely quickly. The Angels have taught me to focus my energy and intentions whenever I see 111 or 1111. Being that the intention of this book was to offer people a simple and easy way to create a consistent, committed meditation practice, I felt as though 111 was the *Perfect* amount of meditations to kickstart a new meditative practice.

Here are some simple steps to start the process if you don't already have your own particular practice. It's simple and easy. No pressure. NO RIGHT way. These are just some helpful guidelines if you are new to meditation or would like to add some new techniques to your practice. Please remember, none of the following guidelines are absolutely necessary – they are just tips that can help you create a great meditative experience for you. Truth be told, the reason I LOVE meditation is I can do it anywhere, anytime with anything or nothing at all.

To Begin:

- Create a space where you will not be interrupted for at least a half hour. No cell phone or computer. Nothing to distract you from the stillness. Make sure this is a safe and comfortable environment for you. You may want to have some sacred objects beside you, such as crystals, deities, incense or a lit candle. It is your space so create it to fit your energy and personality. I would suggest having a journal and a pen beside you for notes afterwards. A computer is fine, but have it off during the meditation.

- Sit in a comfortable position. There are many suggested ways to sit. Many of them are also uncomfortable. Sit in whatever way is comfortable for you … on the floor or on a chair, even laying down is fine. Some people request you to not have your arms or legs crossed; I would suggest to follow your guidance.

- If you feel so guided, take a moment to ask the God of your understanding, your angels, spirit guides or any other spiritual deities for assistance in connecting to the Divine, Source or Spirit. If this is new to you, you can ask Archangel Michael, who helps with maintaining your own energy and/or Archangel Uriel, who helps with seeing the greater vision, for support and guidance.

- Clear your mind. Release the tension from your body. Relax them both by focusing on your breath. I like to use Dr. Andrew Weil's 4-7-8 breathing exercise. You may want to try it, too.

  - ♥ Exhale completely through your mouth, making a whoosh sound.
  - ♥ Close your mouth and inhale quietly through your nose to a mental count of **four**.
  - ♥ Hold your breath for a count of **seven**.
  - ♥ Exhale completely through your mouth, making a whoosh sound to a count of **eight**.
  - ♥ This is one breath.
  - ♥ Now inhale again and repeat the cycle three more times for a total of four breaths

- Now read your meditation for the day. You can go in the order presented in the book, or just open the book randomly to whatever page your Spirit guides you to. Once you have read the meditation, take a few minutes to close your eyes and just observe. Be a witness to your thoughts and feelings. Allow them to just drift in, and out, like clouds. With the thoughts coming in, you are now aware of what is always already there, hidden by the thousands of other thoughts and feelings that you are feeling on a daily basis. The more aware you are, the quieter your mind becomes so that you can really be in touch with the quietness within. As you breathe in and out just let the everyday thoughts drift away, allowing yourself to go deeper within, reaching that stillness where Spirit speaks to you, and reveals any guidance necessary.

- When you feel complete, recharged and present, take a few deep breaths, return back to your space and open your eyes.

- Now take a moment and write down anything that stays with you, anything you feel deep within. This is the guidance of your Spirit. You can do this every day, keeping notes on what the messages are as you continue your meditative journey.

Please remember, with meditation, the more you do it, the deeper you will go and the easier it will become. Practice, practice, practice – and as that stillness comes to you and through you, with commitment and consistency, you will feel a greater connection with Spirit and the guidance within.

Enjoy the journey my friend,

–Sunny Dawn Johnston

1

Protective Blue Bubble

By Sunny Dawn Johnston

In times of challenge, fear and struggle we can all use a little extra support in maintaining our own energy so that we don't become absorbers of the negativity and pain. It is best to do this meditation each morning, before stepping out of bed, or immediately afterwards.

Begin by quieting your body and your mind. Now, visualize a sapphire-blue bubble just in front of you. It is a beautiful vibrating energy: 7 feet high and 4 feet wide. Imagine your physical body standing up and stepping into this beautiful brilliant energy. See and feel your physical self completely embraced by this energy. Now, take a deep breath and feel that energy move through your entire physical body. As you do this, imagine this higher vibrational energy clearing out any negativity, fears or pain that no longer serve you. With each breath you take, see and feel yourself inhaling the protective blue energy, and exhaling any negativity and fear. As you do this, know that you are completely surrounded and protected from any negative energies, thoughts and feelings. Continue this visualization until you feel clear of any negativity.

And so it is.

You do this to strengthen and maintain your own personal energy field – so that it continually revitalizes you throughout the day – not so much to protect yourself from another's negative energies. Others cannot affect you without your allowance. By doing this Blue Bubble meditation, it keeps you proactive and present to the energy within and around you, in each and every day.

2

The Most Important Reminder

By Jean Pomeroy

As I begin my day, I remind myself that the amazing gift of the human experience was not given to me so I could go to the grocery store, take out the garbage, and check off a never-ending to-do list. My reason for being here on Earth, at this time, and in this place, is based on fulfilling my unique life's purpose.

I will spend my day observing what makes me feel enthusiastic, excited and passionate about being alive. Once uncovered, I won't allow negative thoughts to keep me from fulfilling it. I won't allow myself to believe that I don't have the time, the money, or to doubt my success in moving forward with my purpose. Instead, I will speak to everyone who will listen about what lights me up, and my passion to fulfill it. I do not need to know how to get there, because I am aware that by my commitment to fulfill my purpose, the universe will lay the path out for me. I know that in fulfilling my life's purpose, I create a ripple that goes around the world that will inspire others to do the same.

With this reminder, today's to-do list loses its power, and my soul is filled with gratitude for this human experience.

3

Becoming a Beacon of Light
By Lisa Eleni Battaglino-Nelson

As I sit and take deep cleansing breaths to start my day, help me to clear the energy that is no longer serving me. Help me to see the people I cross paths with as a source of your light, and to show up connected to my true essence. Help me interact openly, without barriers and walls.

Allow the hurt feelings or misunderstandings to flow through me so I can feel and learn from the experience. Rather than ignoring my feelings, guide me and allow the stuck energy to flow out of my body, deep into the ground, to be transmuted for my highest good. Help me get out of old patterns of stuffing and replaying my hurts, so I can move to a new understanding of the light that is in all people.

If my interactions today are intended to teach, allow my heart to be open to hear the message and grow. Guide me as I take the necessary steps to become a higher vibration of myself.

If the experiences today are to mirror, help me to recognize what I can learn so I operate and react from your endless source of love and light.

If I am to hold space, allow me to witness and show empathy, compassion and love that connect me to you without having to play my old stories.

As I create my agenda for the day, help me stay focused on my dreams, and connect me on the path of my journey and embrace the day's events. Let my heart be open and willing to receive as I interact with others and move into a new day shining my light.

4

Alleviating Anxiety
By Julie Geigle

Breathe deeply, opening and expanding into all that you are and the beautiful rollercoaster of emotions that continually move you toward awakening and enlightenment.

Move into your body, into your feeling of anxiety. Call in your Spiritual Team to help you manage and mind these free flowing emotions.

How does anxiety feel in your body? Is there a tightness in your chest, a racing in your heart or a feeling of overwhelm?

These are all indicators that anxiety is becoming the predominate force in the experience at the moment.

As you tune into how your body is feeling when anxiety arises, you are able to get a foothold on it before it totally captures and encapsulates you.

If you push through anxiety, it only continues to escalate and become more than you can manage; you are left tired and frustrated; but if you pay attention to your intuition and slowdown in that moment, the feeling will begin to subside.

I want you to imagine with me now, pausing to acknowledge the feelings within your body when anxiety comes on.

Remind yourself that everything is always in perfect and Divine order.

Step out of the future of to-do lists, the past of regrets. Allow yourself to come back into the present where there is perfect order, perfect bliss, perfection always.

Breathe into the present, the beauty this moment has to offer you now. Feel gratitude. Let go of your timelines, for they are only illusions that exist within your mental mind.

In this scope of truth and reality there is always an infinite amount of time to accomplish everything that needs to be done.

I am bathed in a beautiful light-frequency of harmony. Releasing all anxiety and allowing peace to be my predominate driving force.

And so it is.

Channeled meditation by Metatron.

5

A Moment of New Beginnings

By Carolan Dickinson

Every day is an opportunity for new beginnings. Let this be your day. Get comfortable and ready to meditate. Close your eyes and ask the angels to surround you. Take any worry, fear, concern, or the "to do" lists, and place them in a box. Give this box to your angels. The box, and everything inside of it, are gone forever. The angels have taken it to a place where no retrieval is possible. Breathe in and breathe out several times, feeling the stillness and quiet void. Here you find your center; you are at peace. Bring your awareness to your breath and allow your exhales to carry away any thoughts about the past, yesterday, or even a second ago. Breathe in freshness, forgiveness, and joy. In this sacred space, hear, see, and feel any messages your angels have for you.

Envision a light as bright as a million stars on a moonlit night, sparkling as a small ball in your solar plexus. Allow it to turn and rotate, radiating there for a few breaths. Feel its warmth comfort you. As the light expands, it creates space through your hips, legs, and feet. This light continues to spread as it travels up your midsection, creating space in your lungs, heart, third eye, and crown. It fills every tiny cell inside of you until it spills over and illuminates your etheric body. Bask in the energy as it flows through you. You are reborn. Embrace this feeling of beginning again. As you move through your day, know that you can return here; simply breathe in this moment of new beginnings.

6

Close Your Eyes, and Believe!

By Bonnie Larson

In your morning space of appreciation, close your eyes. Breathe.

Quiet your mind. Inhale deeply, infusing your body with the
breath of the Spirit.

Exhale all that troubles you, all the concerns of the material world.

Know that you are loved. Breathe.

You are love, the passion of our Creator.

Invite the light to you, through you, releasing all doubt. Breathe.

You are love. You are light. You are beautiful. Believe.

You are the consummate balance of the feminine and masculine,
complementary aspects.

You are a perfect child of grace, faith, and compassion. Marry your gifts
with the Divine.

The Spirit descends, as you ascend, meeting in the middle, at zero point.

Rejoice! Know that you are loved. Know that you are light.

Transcend the limitations of the physical. Know that you are.

You are healthy, vibrant, a lighted vessel. A beacon of light, attracting
light, illuminating light.

You are a consciousness of higher vibration.

Bring the light through your crown,

Your third eye,

Your voice,

Your heart center,

Solar plexus,

Base,

Knees,

And feet.

See the light passing through you, grounding you as it progresses
into the soil beneath you.

As the light continues, see it infusing Mother Earth
with healing regeneration.

Feel the joy of the higher vibration, lighting your energy centers,
your circuits, your cells.

You are light. You are love, in all that you do.

Feel the Source replenish your body.

The gentleness, softness of our Mother;

Her essence breath, breathed for us.

Whole again, you feel refreshed, energized and ready to start your day.

Hold this glowing feeling for a few more minutes.

You are satisfied, appreciative, filled with love.

As you return to consciousness, remember that this feeling of
Love Divine is easily accessible.

Simply close your eyes, and believe!

7

Meditation to Help You Ground with Mother Earth

By Georgia Nagel

Find your quiet, comfortable space. Sitting upright or lying down, close your eyes, take a deep breath, then release that breath. As you breathe in and out, begin to feel your body relax. Imagine a white light entering in through the top of your head, working its way through your body and out of your feet, connecting you to Mother Earth.

As you relax, see yourself walking on a path; there are tall trees and you can smell the earth and feel the cool air as you walk under this canopy of trees. In the distance, you see an open area with taller grasses and wild flowers blooming in yellow, white, blue and purple colors. As you approach that area, you hear what sounds like running water. On the edge of this grassy area is a small stream; water slowly trickling over the rocks of all sizes. You take off your shoes and step into the stream. The water is cold at first but feels so refreshing. It feels good slowly trickling over your feet. You cannot believe how clear the water is.

Something catches your eye; you reach down to pick it up. It is a stone in the shape of a heart; it feels smooth in your hand. You climb out of the stream and lay on a patch of lush, green grass; it envelops your body. You place the stone over your heart; you can feel the energy of the stone. This stone is vibrating in rhythm with your heart. It feels like you and the stone have the same heartbeat. You are grounded with Mother Earth.

You slowly get up, place the stone back in the stream, thanking the stone. You walk back through the grassy field and under the canopy of trees, now returning to your home.

8

Tree Meditation
By Ann Albers

Leaning against a big ponderosa pine, she taught me this meditation to connect myself with earth and sky, and all else around me.

Imagine – You stand with your back to a tall pine tree in the middle of a pristine forest. There is a gentle warmth and a slight breeze. The birds are singing. You hear the slight gurgling of a creek nearby. You and the tree are going to breathe together. She will help you reach a deep and peaceful space, connecting you with heaven, earth, and all of life around you.

Take a deep breath in, as if you could inhale through your roots, through the soles of your feet, drawing energy up from the earth into your heart. Exhale as you release the energy through the top of your head.
Imagine its movement.

Breathe again, as if you could inhale from the top of your head, drawing the heavenly energies down into your heart, and exhaling downward through the soles of your feet.

Continue like this, inhaling the earth energies, exhaling to the heavens; inhaling the heavenly energies, and exhaling into the earth. Be rhythmical and relaxed. Focus on your breath and the movement of energy through your body.

After a while you may realize that you are no longer controlling the direction of the energy. You are drawing energy and breath in from all around you, as if you could inhale the essence of forest and life itself into every pore; as if with each exhale, you could gift them back with the very essence of your being.

Breathe in, imagining taking in energy from all directions. Breathe out, offering it back to life. Continue in this fashion relaxed, and rhythmical, your back to the pine tree, a gentle breeze upon your skin. Peace.

9

Finding Calm Amidst Chaos
By Julie Geigle

Take a nice deep breath, stepping into this beautiful, sacred space and opening to receive the beautiful Divine order that is here to help you now.

As you open your heart and invite this beautiful message in, it allows a beautiful healing within your soul, your spirit, your human self.

There is much occurring on your planet at this time. The energies may be turbulent as the old falls away and the new begins to rise up.

Out of chaos comes order; out of unrest comes peace.

You are a Lightworker and your Spiritual team is here to help you remember where your power lies. Envision God, the Divine source energy, your angels and guides surrounding you and enfolding you in their love and joy.

Do not get caught up in the drama of the world. Allow yourself to stay grounded, sure-footed, ever expansive.

It is in this energy, in your alignment with the earth and the universe that you will gain your power. Allow this energy to come forth into the chaos, remembering always that you are a Lightworker.

Imagine standing strong as a Lightworker and becoming one with the light that you are.

Now feel yourself standing inside a LIGHTHOUSE, confident and secure, allowing your light to shine upon the world, upon your inner circle of family and friends.

There is nothing that can hurt you, there is nothing to fear, for you have a forcefield of love and light around you and within you that is impenetrable.

You are not powerless amidst the chaos; you are powerful.

You are a Lightworker and your LIGHT is your super power.

Channeled meditation by Metatron.

10

Body Balance Meditation
By Michelle Beltran

I love my body just as it is. My body is aligned and balanced at all times.

I release resistance of any kind surrounding my body now. My physical body blossoms as I release any resistance.

I am making mental lists each day of all the things I love about my body. Body balance is my birthright.

Every aspect of my body, every atom and every cell, is whole and complete.

There is a profound rejuvenation of all the cells of my body beyond my comprehension.

Past or unwanted issues leave my body now. I begin to feel the power that flows through me with this releasing.

Every morning, before I start my day, I take a few moments to appreciate my perfect body. I end my day in the same way.

I am _____ (fill in blank) and I love my body fully and completely.

As I allow my body to come alive, I feel an unleashing of magnificent energy.

My body's natural way is one of well-being. I thank my body now. Vitality exudes from every cell of my body.

I am in my body now. I am present with my body now. I love my body.

I am creating a balanced body that feels right to me.

The cells of my body are healthy and well. I relax into and accept this truth.

Physical well-being is easy for me to sustain. My alignment with this knowing grows stronger every day.

There is no need to try to find body balance. It comes to me effortlessly, with love and grace.

There is a Divine plan, far greater than me, bringing health and well-being to me now. I trust in this with all that I AM.

11

Be Here Now

By Jani Metzger McCarty

Begin this morning's meditation by
placing your feet shoulder width apart.
Reach your arms fully to the heavens while taking a deep Breath.
Exhale completely as you lower your arms, elbows first,
into a cactus or goal post position.
Sink your shoulders down and hold in the release of your Breath.
Repeat two more times.
Notice how your chest and heart space openly embrace each Breath.

Now settle into your chair or the floor, close your eyes,
and relax in this new position.
Allow your hands to fall to your lap comfortably, without touching.
Notice the rhythm of your regular Breathing,
Notice how your body feels…
Give yourself permission to release any thoughts or tight energy perhaps
surfacing from the previous night or the day to come.

Consciously begin to inhale deeply through your nose.
Hold each Breath for 2-3 counts, then while making an audible "sigh"
sound, exhale through your open mouth. Repeat three times.

Relax … Breathe!
Focus your awareness on your centeredness.
Notice how grounded and safe you feel.
Be present and conscious of your Life in this Breath,
in this now moment…
Breathe. Here.

Dr. Robert Holden reminds us that:
*"Grace is the awareness that Life is ALWAYS lived in the present
And that getting there really means, Being Here…"*

And in your present awareness, Breathe deep into your heart space.
Allow the wholeness of who you are to move into alignment
with your heart.
Notice how your Breath accompanies the rhythm of your heart.
Notice how your heart welcomes each Breath.
Rest in your awareness of grace in this moment.
Breathe…

Give yourself permission to sink deep into your heart's warm welcome.
Gently pull its downy comfort around your shoulders.
Breathe…

Trust in the knowing of your Sacred connection!
Celebrate!

Be Here … Now!

12

Gratitude in Manifesting

By Dr. Karen Maxwell

Close your eyes. Take in a slow deep breath, hold, then slowly release. Do this a few more times. Allow your whole body to relax. Release any tension you may be holding on to. As you begin to notice the slow rhythm of your breath coming in, think about all the things you are grateful for: your breath, life, family, home, pets, career, abundance, even your refrigerator. As you breathe out, let go of all those things that no longer serve you: an unfinished project, the argument you had with your friend, the driver that cut you off, the headline news.

Now allow your mind to be free by just letting go of your thoughts and begin to repeat silently your activating thought for the day, *"Gratefulness is the magical process in manifesting all my desires."* Repeat this affirmation three times and allow the silence to envelop you.

If noises, thoughts or body sensations disrupt you, gently bring yourself back to your activating thought, *"Gratefulness is the magical process in manifesting all my desires."*

Sit in silence for as long as you can. Don't try to force anything, stay in a state of relaxation and gratitude.

When you are ready, release your activating thought, wiggle your toes, stretch and slowly open your eyes.

Manifestation is always your perception and your vibrational interpretation. The more you are grateful for the things that you have in your life, the more you will manifest, and thus, become more grateful. Think only of the best feeling thought you have in regards to what you wish to manifest. A belief is only a thought you continue to think, and when your beliefs match your desires, then your desires must become your manifestations. Gratitude is the magical process to manifesting all of your desires.

13

Master Your Day
By Kyra Schaefer, CHT

Take a deep breath and exhale with the sound of "Ahhhhh."
Repeat three times. Yawn, stretch and embrace the day.

Repeat these words to yourself out loud:

"I am in harmony with the world around me."

"No matter what happens today, I will choose a loving response."

"I am needed in this world. I trust myself."

"I can change the circumstances of my life, by seeing them differently."

"I am enjoying the possibility of a new outcome."

"I am learning to love myself better."

"Today, I will celebrate my successes, no matter how small."

Reach your spirit and thoughts out into your day. Discover the places of
possible disconnection and visualize a beautiful light working its way
through those potential challenges. Let that light transform difficulty into
triumph. This day is yours to discover; fill it, make it your own.
You are the master of your creation.

14

I Choose to Remember

By Michelle McDonald Vlastnik

In meditation, I asked my Soul to give me a word. She gave me *OWNness*. I pondered ... and this was my unfolding. OWNness: Own your Shit. Own your Shift. Own your Truth. Own your Vibe, especially in your Tribe. Vibe your Truth in ALL spaces and places because that is what Being Authentic is.

I looked into the meaning of "ness" for a deeper understanding and to fully grasp the knowledge of what my Soul was reflecting. Ness: The State of Being. The Quality of Being. The Measure of Being. OWNness became the creed for my Authentic Self and living on Purpose.

Let's meditate and get you a word from your Soul to ponder...
Connecting in breath, I sit in centered stillness.
My quest is my Truth, moving me into Wholeness.

Help me align with my Authentic foundation,
solid in Self-Love—the true way of creation.

I collapse Timelines that no longer serve me this day.
I declare them dissolved, for this is the New Earth way.

I choose to remember, the illusion I do not OWN!
I call forth the Knowing of my Frequency Tone.

Ask your Soul: *What word do you have to give me today?*

Ponder this perspective... We are Human Beings. We are Light Beings. In Wholeness, we are no longer living as two parts. Through our remembrance, our higher vibration brings into form the body needed to hold the merging of our balanced s/Selves. When we are living in harmonious Divine alignment, our Higher Self/Mind is operating in physical form. As each of us arrives here, we will be experiencing Heaven on Earth through our expansion with All That Is. They call this place the New Earth.

Ask your Soul: *What Divine reflection can you bring forth for me?*

15

My Gift to God

By Rosemary Hurwitz

Today, when I get short or critical with others, let me remember, "It's not always my problem," and "Let go and let God."

Today, when I have difficulty with either giving or receiving, let me remember that it is in both the receiving and the giving that I find my true balance and feel empowered.

Today, when I may go on overdrive or work too hard, and get caught up with my image instead of what I truly feel, let me remember that acknowledging my feelings will lead me to my inner truth.

Today, when I long for things or even envy someone, let me remember, I have everything I need in this moment to grow. Let me begin to reach my dreams with baby steps.

Today, when I withhold myself from others or stay in my cave too long collecting information, let me remember, shared experiences are often the best teacher for us all.

Today, when I second-guess myself or mistrust another too quickly, let me remember that you, my Divine source and force are always with me, guiding me to my inner authority and knowing.

Today, when I want to consume too much or take on too much, let me know that focus is my holy work, and less can be more. I only need to breathe and slow down the train and then I can make my healthy choice.

Today, when I feel the need to be strong all the time, let me know your tender mercies for my vulnerabilities.

Today, when I want to run away from any tensions or conflicts, let me remember, resolving little problems can prevent bigger problems.

Thank you for your constant support in my journey. I only need to breathe into your guidance in any trouble spots and you are there.

16

Start Your Day the Light Filled Way
By Marla Steele

I start my day the light filled way.
Breathing in the breath of God,
Breathing out the love of Jesus.
As a vessel of your light and love,
I trust I will always be in the right place
at the right time to best be of service.
Breathe in the pure white light allowing it to cleanse and replenish.

I attract the people, animals and situations that are a divine match for me.
I recognize when it is time to take action by the impulse in my heart
and the time to be patient by the hesitation in my body.
Think of a situation and imagine a red light or green light.

I know who I AM.
I AM clear and congruent in my energy.
I release attachments to others
and return to a space of neutrality.
*Invoke Archangel Michael to help you cut any fear
or lack-based cords of energy.*

I know where I AM going.
I AM led by my team of angels, guides and spirit animals.
I create space each day to notice their signs, symbols
and messages of love.
Like this one right now_____.

I know where I AM growing.
I listen to my soul,
Honoring the wisdom of my heart
and the expansive power of my mind.

I surround myself with the conditions that I want to create
and I know that I am already connected to everything I need and desire.
Send beams of purple light out for manifestations.

Feeling the love that I AM,
I give a soul-to-soul hello to all of the beings I will encounter today.
Send a beautiful rose quartz bubble to each one.

Together we shall unite, shine bright and share the magic of life.

Thank you, thank you, thank you!
Breathe and radiate a bright golden essence.

17

A Feather on the Breath of God
By Adriana C. Tomasino

Please close your eyes and breathe deeply into a place of peace …
As you feel the healing warmth of the Sun on your face, envision
yourself traveling upon the grand winged steed Pegasus to visit
Hildegard von Bingen on her feast day …

Upon alighting, and thanking Pegasus for guiding you safely, you meet
Hildegard … After exchanging pleasantries, she gestures for you to come
to her ethereal medieval garden filled with the delights of heart and soul
that are a feast for the senses; colors rivaling those in the most glorious
rainbow … scents of lavender and honeysuckle, wafting in the breeze …
sounds of the "music of the spheres" reverberating in the melodious
serenity that surrounds you—and that exist in your
own Sacré-Cœur …

As you emerge from your reverie, Hildegard smiles and asks you to be
seated upon a stone bench, among others, encircling a large labyrinth …
She suggests we honor and bless where we are, individually and
collectively, as we walk the spiral path standing before us … At our
center—and that within the labyrinth, is the ceremonial fire of
purification—one that does not burn, but illuminates as a
Divine Spark from within …

Hildegard speaks to our reason for being here—at this gathering—and on
Planet Earth at this crucial time. She continues, "I [am] a feather on the
breath of God," as are each of you … "Remember to reflect upon the
stillness of water as that is who and what you are—a timeless being
whose birthright resides in the very Oneness of the Universe …
Fare thee well …"

After you exchange "goodbyes," you thank Pegasus for the gift of flight.
On your way home, you feel the coolness of the Moon's iridescent
beams upon your face—and with each breath, you more fully return
to your awakened state …

18

Your Daily Guidance for Self-Confidence
By Misty Proffitt-Thompson

Be the light your Creator longed for you to be. Building your self-confidence will shine that light for the world to witness and follow. Believe that you are worthy, because you most certainly are. Take small steps so you do not feel overwhelmed.

Read each affirmation below daily, then pick at least one as a guidance for you to follow throughout your day. Before bed, take time to journal your lessons, signs and validations. No outcome is wrong as you will learn exactly what you need from each encounter. Please look at your experiences in a positive way, no matter the result.

Be patient with yourself, for we all are a work in progress. As you read each affirmation, slow down and savor the words you are reading. Take a deep breath before moving on to the next. Remember that you are not alone, for God and his Angels are with you always!!

*I am open to receive love.

*I schedule time for my self-care.

*I am present throughout my day to witness signs from the Angels and the beauty around me.

*I am learning about areas that I find interesting, as I know it will bring me power.

*I find inspiration in all that I encounter.

*I awaken my creative side by writing, coloring, dancing and singing.

*I take time to exercise.

*I will take time to be outside in nature to breathe in fresh air.

*I show my vulnerability instead of hiding behind my feelings.

*I take time to eat food that is nourishing to my body.

*I show gratitude and appreciation for the kindness that others display.

*I am worthy to receive abundance.

*I am exactly where I need to be at this moment for my higher good.

*I am confident.

19

Rainbow Bridge: The Bridge to Center
By Shalini Saxena Breault

This may be done either standing or sitting. Begin by planting your feet firmly on the ground hip distance apart. Tuck your tailbone in with your spine straight. Take a few purposeful deep inhalations and gentle slow exhalations. Connect to an intention, mantra, or prayer you would like to focus on for the day.

Plant your feet firmly on Mother Earth. Imagine roots going down from the soles of your feet to the depths of Mother Earth. Bring to mind something you would like to let go of. Offer it to Mother Earth and allow her to heal and nourish you. Feel the earth energy in and around you.

Move your awareness up the soles of your feet, up both your legs, to just below your navel. Gently breathe in and out a juicy orange color. Imagine you can create anything you desire today – what would that be? Create all possibilities here. Let your imagination run wild and free.

Move your awareness up above your navel. Gently breathe in and out a bright sunny yellow color. Connect to your fire energy here. Know you are a warrior who stands up strong with confidence and grace. Feel the fire energy move in and around you.

Now, move your awareness to the crown of your head. Connect to your Source. Call in your Angels, Guides, Ascended Masters, or loved ones to join you today for guidance and company.

Move your awareness down to the area between your eyebrows. Gently breathe in and out an indigo color. See your intention, mantra or prayer in your mind's eye. Visualize it … feel it … embody it …

Move your awareness down to the throat area. Gently breathe in and out a sky blue color. What do you desire to express today? Know you are supported to express your truth with love and confidence.

Breathing up from the soles of your feet and down from the crown of your head, you will meet at your heart center. Gently breathe in and out a sparkly emerald green color. Feel peace, harmony and balance running down both your arms into your palms. Bow in gratitude.

20

Beautiful, Boundless, Bliss

By Tonia Browne

Close your eyes and as you breathe in,
be aware of your breath and your thoughts.
As you breathe out,
place your attention more on your breath
and let your thoughts disperse.
Anything of importance can be visited again - later.
For this is your time.
As you breathe in, notice how this replenishes you.
And as you breathe out, allow the air to escape
as if it has all the time in the world,
leaving you lighter.
With each breath, become aware that your world is slowing down
and that you are merging with the space and energy around you.
This state feels good.
Notice the stillness, the completeness, the love
and become aware that you feel more peaceful.
Allow yourself to feel it
and accept it as a gift.
Begin to feel a stirring of excitement of all that is possible
and of all that can be.
Breathe in again,
deeper now,
filling your whole being with this energy of love.
Feel your vibration rising,
and as you do,
notice it radiate from you.
Let it ease your body, your mind and your spirit
and beam out into your world.
Then, when you feel it is time,
bring your attention back to your breath and
also back to your physical plane.

Slowly open your eyes and smile,
for you have chosen to feel joy
and have helped to start your day
from a place of bliss.
Beautiful, boundless, bliss.

21

Your Energy Rejuvenation
By Kelli Lee Sappenfield

Stand up straight and tall, feet firmly planted, hands open, bringing your focus into your feet. Envision the soles of your feet taking root into Mother Earth. See and feel your roots descending to the earth's core. Feel the energy spinning there, burning up what no longer serves you and creating fuel for your rebirth.

Now bring that new, cleansing Universal energy up through your roots and into your feet.

Feel it flowing up your legs and into your torso, through your shoulders, and down your arms.

See it ascending to your neck, into your head, and up to your crown. Open your crown chakra, raising your attention up through it, seeing and feeling the Divine white-light energy.

Now, notice the Divine light enveloping your entire energetic being, filling and cleansing away all negative energy, washing over you in gentle energetic waves.

Bring that pure Divine energy into your body through your crown. Feel it flowing into your consciousness, filling every cell.

See this energy pouring down your neck, shoulders, arms, and flowing out of your fingertips.

This superabundance of energy fills your chest, until your heart beams with pure Divine love and joy.

See it overflowing into your abdomen, hips, legs, and feet, down into your roots, cascading once again to Mother Earth's core. Watch as it mixes with her Universal energy and creates an infinite cycling of energies, rising through your roots and into your body, shooting up through your crown into the Divine white light. Then it reverses course and flows back again. Feel and see this current cleansing and refilling every cell of your physical and spiritual body with optimal energy.

When you feel completely renewed, bring your roots back in, close your crown chakra, and come home to your heart, taking a few deep breaths.

22

Gifts from Heaven

By Carolan Dickinson

You are loved more than air, and more than anything measurable. In those times when you feel alone, know that you are so loved that God created the angels to be with you and to walk this life with you, in every second of every day. Close your eyes and prepare for meditation. As you breathe in and out, relax into each breath; feel God's love embrace you.

Allow your thoughts to take you to a quiet beach with the sun just visible on the horizon. You stand with your feet at the water's edge. Every time the water retreats, it takes with it something that no longer serves you. When the water returns, it rushes over your feet, bringing to you the one thing your heart wants more than anything: love. A deeply satisfying, angelic, heavenly-sent agape love that fills you from your crown to your toes. You feel this love spread across your chest like warm honey; knowing that heaven is the only place this kind of love comes from.

Archangel Chamuel stands next to you sending rose pink energy to your heart, filling it up front and back. Slowly, this rose pink energy of unconditional love flows throughout your entire being. You feel heaven's embrace and know that you are never alone. You are totally and completely loved. Archangel Chamuel takes your hands, placing something in your palm, closing your fist around it. Archangel Chamuel puts an arm around your shoulders, embracing you as you stand on the beach looking at the horizon. You feel completely loved, as you open your palm to receive your gift.

23

Manifest the Relationship
You Desire, Now

By Michelle Beltran

I am appreciative of all the things in my life now.

I cannot manifest anything into reality by noticing what is missing. I shift
my attention to noticing only what I desire.

I am making mental lists each day of all the things I love in my life,
from the shoes on my feet to my health and wellbeing.

With great detail and deep feeling, I imagine this soulmate present in my
life now. I act as if they are here now.

We laugh wildly together and tears of joy flow from our eyes.

I am in a deep-seated, loving relationship with a
uniquely wonderful person. I feel fulfilled.

Every morning, before I start my day, I take a few moments to appreciate
everything I have now. I end my day in the same way.

I am _____ and I love myself fully.

I can do, be or have anything I so desire. I know this to be true.

I am aligning with my Higher Self.
I understand that no one completes me. I complete me.

My thoughts are far more powerful than my actions. As I give thought to
the love I desire, it comes to me fully. I relax into this knowing.

I am excited about what is to come in my life. Life is not happening to me; I am creating it. I am creating this meaningful soulmate relationship.

I expect and intend this relationship. I release resistance.
I accept it and allow it to come now.

There is no need to try. It is only a matter of time now.
It is only a matter of when, not if.

There is a divine plan far greater than me
bringing this soulmate to me now. I trust in this.

24

Inspiration from Loved Ones
By Susan Luth Leahey

Relax in a space that makes you feel cozy and safe. Let your breath remove anything in your body that's not serving you today. Take a deep breath in, letting go of those things you no longer need; feel them drop out of your pores and experience the lightness that soothes and calms your spirit. In this lightness, you can feel your body float; floating to the bright light that awaits you above. Notice the color of the light and the beam that is connected to it. Travel along this beam to your perfect spot. Sit and take in the fragrance of the air and the beauty that surrounds you.

Settle in, and notice you are suddenly no longer alone. Others have joined you in your beautiful space; they surround you in a circle. You feel a warming sense of love and support from all of them. They are your family; the same angels and guides who have been with you throughout your life. Take a moment and bask in the strength of unconditional love you feel from them. You hold hands, you smile, and you feel a sense of wonder and peace. After a moment, one of them has a message for you. Listen to your message. Who is it and what do they want you to know? Ask if anyone else has a message for you today.

It is time to leave, and you embrace your loved ones; they remind you they are always with you. Take a few more moments to thank them and return to the present. Make a memory marker of your experience and know that you are loved and supported today, and every day.

25

Start Each Day with an Open Heart
By Robin Lynn Harned

Good Morning to All My Angels, Guides and Helpers!

Thank you for this beautiful day
and for all of the wonderful things you always bring my way!

Thank you for the peace in my heart and the joy that lies within my soul.

As I move through my day,

I ask that you clear from my body, my mind and my spirit
any and all negative energies, or entities, seen or unseen…

So I may be of service in the best way in which you deem fit!

And So It Is.

Namasté

26

Rise and Shine
By Deb Alexander

I invite you to sit quietly and anticipate the day, by closing your eyes and taking nice deep, even breaths, in and out through your nose.

Breathe deep within your belly, letting any thoughts of the day ahead come into your mind and leave, staying in the presence of peace.

As the morning sun rises in the East, so let your soul come to life, singing to the morning a new song, full of Love, Light, and Laughter.

Feel the lightness of your body, as a new day begins.

Feel the energy from the warmth of the sun, upon your face and body, embracing your skin like a warm blanket.

Feel the Energy of a gentle breeze, as it whispers hope for the day and brushes love against your skin.

Feel the energy surround you.

Feel the energy of your breath as it awakens every cell of your Being, from the top of your head to the tip of your toes.

Behold, your senses become alive and react with every breath that you take, saying to you softly, "Rise and Shine".

Your day has begun.
The journey of your life awaits you.

27

Today I Will Take a Moment to Be Silent
By Sandy Turkington

Today, I silence the noise of my mind; I stop listening to my ego and the influence of others. In doing this, I become aware of my senses; to hear, to feel, and to touch. In this beautiful silence, my inner voice becomes clear as I listen to it. Truth and love move forward, removing all fear and doubt. My trust becomes stronger, as I know you are with me, every step of the way. You and I are one, and I thank you.

"To hear, one must be silent."
~ Ursula K. Le Guin

28

Awaiting Dawn

By Lindsley Silagi

In the darkness you begin. You find a place to sit outside in the still dark of the early morning hour. You take a deep breath, and slowly let the air out. You take another deep breath; you allow the air to fill your chest. And then you slowly let this air out. You bring yourself to a place of calm. Then you listen to the sounds around you. What do you hear? Do you hear the Whip-poor-will calling high above on the branch of a sycamore tree? Do you hear its sweet song? It is waiting, too, for Dawn. You are not alone in your wait for Dawn. Do you feel the cool air and the oh-so-gentle breeze? This is goodness, you think to yourself. You drink it in like cool water. You breathe now. You breathe deeply, filling your lungs and emptying them. You breathe in, out, in, out.

Now you notice that the dark sky is beginning to lighten up ever so slowly. You rise up ever so slowly, too. You begin to walk slowly up a path that leads you to a staircase. You climb the steps one at a time. You feel supported as you climb higher. At the top is a lookout area with a slab of sandstone for a seat. You sit once more. You breathe in, out, in, out. The sky is brighter now, and you take notice of this. You realize that soon you can claim that Dawn has arrived. You wait. You breathe. You take in the sounds at this new place, this higher ground. And then you find that Dawn has come. Yes, Dawn!

You breathe in again and arise to take the journey down the staircase and into your new day, ready, refreshed.

29

Starting My Day the Miraculous Way
By Renée Essex-Spurrier

Today is a fresh new day! I can create something different than ever before. There are 24 hours of endless possibilities! I am excited about the day ahead.

I begin my day by connecting to Source and being appreciative for all that I have.

I am deeply grateful for:

♥ My bed that helped me sleep comfortably all night.

♥ My home that provides me shelter and safety.

♥ The water that cleanses and refreshes me as I wake and prepare for my day.

♥ Each person/animal I love (name them and smile as you think of their unique soul qualities and how they touch your life).

♥ Each situation I'm going through right now, 'good' or 'bad', as I know that all situations are really there to serve me and my spiritual growth.

♥ My health, for even if parts of me aren't well, I can focus this moment on the parts of me that are.

♥ My work and the money that I do or do not have, as I trust that I will always be provided for.

♥ My gifts and talents, that I may share them confidently with the world and recognize my awesomeness.

♥ All the love in my life past, present and in the future.

♥ All my blessings.

Find the strongest point of light wherever you are, where the Divine can enter your heart most powerfully, and stand facing it with your arms outstretched and say:

♥ I am open and receptive to even more good.

♥ Please guide me in everything I say and do today.

♥ This is going to be a great day. I wonder what miracles will happen today?!

Now go out and enjoy a beautiful day, expecting miracles and wonderful surprises and synchronicities along the way!

30

Morning Forgiveness Meditation

By Angela N. Holton

Sit or lie in a comfortable and relaxed position.

Bring both hands, palms flat, over your heart and begin to breathe slowly and deeply.

Allow the breath to flow steadily, in through the nose, holding the breath in for a few seconds; and then gently, with control, exhaling out through the nose.

Feel the breath as it flows gently through the body, paying close attention to the breath as it passes through the lungs and chest.

Imagine the breath as a white light surrounding your heart. With each breath, imagine that light becoming bolder and brighter as it fills up your heart.

Bring the energy of love and compassion into your heart. Conjure up as much love and equanimity into your heart as you can.

Keep breathing deeply into your heart until you feel your vibration lifted.

With your hands over your heart, begin to slowly repeat in your mind's eye:

I forgive myself. I forgive myself. I forgive myself.

I forgive myself for every bad thought I have ever held onto.

I forgive myself for every negative emotion that has hurt me.

I forgive myself for judging and criticizing myself and others.

I forgive myself for any harm I have ever caused myself and others.

I forgive myself and I set myself free!

Notice your heart soften and expand.

Now visualize forgiveness as a white light of love that extends out from your heart and out into the world.

Visualize yourself sending this light of compassion to the people around you today and to anyone you want to forgive. Imagine them surrounded in this white light and your heart filling with compassion.

Carry the light of compassion and love within your heart throughout the day today!

31

Meditation of Gratitude, Love, Peace, Joy & Trust

By Kris Groth

In this moment, I breathe and connect with my deepest self,
the earth and the Divine.

Feeling gratitude for the gift of this day. Grateful to be alive, healthy and
whole. Grateful for the beauty that is before me. Grateful for all
abundance coming my way. Grateful for the miracles in every moment.
I am grateful!

Love flows through me for all that is in my life. Love for myself and all
that I am. Love for the earth and all living creatures. Love for humanity
and all the universe. Love radiates all around me. I am Love!

Peace fills my entire being. With each breath, I breathe in peace. Peace in
my body as I am calm and relaxed. Peace in my heart as I am
compassionate. Peace in my mind as I let go of worry. Peace in my soul
as I embrace my truth and my purpose. I am at peace!

Joy surrounds me as I anticipate the magic this day holds. Joyful to see
the beautiful displays of nature unfolding. Joyful to play and dance,
celebrating the gift of life. Joyful for the blessings all around me.
I am joyful!

Cultivating trust in all areas of my life. Trust in myself and my intuition,
seeing clearly the truth of what I sense and know. Trusting I will find
light in darkness and blessings in challenges. Trusting the divine, all my
prayers will be answered in unexpected and miraculous ways.
Trusting all will be well. I have trust!

My intention for today is to live my day in connection to my soul and my
truth. All of my thoughts, words and actions reflect who I truly am and
radiate gratitude, love, peace, joy and trust to all around me.
Today is an amazing day!

32

Create an Energetic Pathway
By Maggie Chula

As I breathe in the breath of life from the source of all that is, I allow my thoughts to be brightened by the vibration of love that enters as I breathe.

I see this breath of life entering my body, filling up my lungs with light, love and peace.

As I continue to breathe, I know this light vibration is flowing all the way through my body, igniting my cells with the vibrational energy of life.

I know this heavenly vibration is expanding outward from the center of my being. Extending up into the heart of my soul. Extending down into the heart of the Earth.

I am aware my heavenly team of guides and angels surround me and welcome me to come and play with them today.

I acknowledge this invitation, and I ask them to stay with me and help me.

Help me know when my thoughts and energy are being pulled away from my chosen goals so I may stay on track and on time.

Help me acknowledge signs from spirit and know I have been heard; I am supported.

Help me relax and breathe when I feel anxious or upset.

I accept my part in the creation of my life. I acknowledge my choices. I invite compassion into my heart so my choices are made with thought for what is the highest and best for all concerned.

I am ready, now. I am ready to start my day and stay in the loving guidance of my soul.

33

Today, I Am Enough – Today, I Am Love

By Rev. Jamie Lynn Thompson

With deep, slow breaths, I am surrounded by the white light of love and protection. I breathe in Love. Today, I am Love. Today, I am protected.

Today, I am Enough! Today, I am Love!

I bless and thank the North, the Mother Earth and my physical body. We are one. We are love.

Today, I am Enough! Today, I am Love!

I bless and thank the East, the Divine, my Father and the air I breathe. The air is my Divine essence from the Divine, My Spirit. We are one. We are love.

Today, I am Enough! Today, I am Love!

I bless and thank the South, the sun fire and the son, the light of the world. The light of my soul. We are one. We are love.

Today, I am Enough! Today, I am Love!

I bless and thank the West, the waters, the Holy Spirit and the Angels. As vast as my thoughts and my emotions. We are one. We are love.

Today, I am Enough! Today, I am Love!

I bless and thank the Faith Wheel, the complete circle of life. We are one. We are love.

Today, I am Enough! Today, I am Love!

34

A Meditation to Connect With Your Inner~Butterfly

By Katrina L. Wright

Gently close your eyes and take a deep breath in. And then slowly breathe out. Repeat this four times. Connect with a consistent sound in your environment that elicits a state of inner~calm and peace.

Silently repeat to yourself:

"I bow down to the grace that dwells within me, and the love which is forever flowing through me and to me, in every way. I am the Light of pure, positive energy. My body renders the weightlessness of a beautiful butterfly whose wings are of crimson red. I am filled with sheer exuberance and enthusiasm for what the day has in store for me. I honor this moment of connection to my own divinity and to who I truly am. I allow the feelings that emerge from within me now to simply just be. I feel the full expansion of my heart, like the wings of my crimson red butterfly, growing upon each breath. I know and trust that no matter how my day unfolds, or whatever unexpected course it may take, that everything is going to be alright ... for God, The Universe, Spirit, Source~Energy, my Angels & Guides, Ascended Masters, Friends and Loved Ones from the other side of the rainbow bridge are always here supporting me and have my back. It's already a beautiful day!"

35

I AM (AHAM) Meditation
By Sarah Auger

Sit comfortably and take five deep breaths, releasing slowly as you exhale, while visualizing the release of anything and everything that does not serve you in this moment.

Repeat "AHAM" (Sanskrit for "I AM") 10 times silently, and with your eyes closed.

Notice the energy shift in your body as you let go and allow the energy of who you really are to be present. Continue to FEEL this energy as you move through the meditation effortlessly and slowly. Become familiar with the I AM energy and tap into it at any time throughout your day.

I AM love. AHAM.
I AM power. AHAM.
I AM free. AHAM.
I AM a wonderful creator. AHAM.
I AM stepping into my truth. AHAM.
I AM boundless. AHAM.
I AM filled with divine light. AHAM.
I AM a receiver of divine guidance. AHAM.
I AM always connected to my Source. AHAM.
I AM. AHAM.

Opportunities are always flowing to me. AHAM.
My divine light is always present, always accessible. AHAM.
My divine purpose is revealed to me now. AHAM.
Source energy lights my path. I now step forward fearlessly. AHAM.
Abundance surrounds me and is overflowing. AHAM.
Perceived obstacles crumble, vanish and are now released from my being. AHAM.

Divine solutions are instantly revealed to me. AHAM.
Untruths are now released from my subconscious. AHAM.
I accept love in all of its forms. AHAM.
Divine timing guides my life. AHAM.
I trust. I believe. I know. AHAM.
I AM. AHAM.

I AM grateful. AHAM.
I AM blessed. AHAM.
I AM a knower of all divine truths. AHAM.
I AM of the highest vibration. AHAM.
I AM healed. AHAM.
I AM peace. AHAM.
I AM whole. AHAM.
I AM resting. I AM being.
I AM love.
I AM. AHAM.

36

The Rainbow Bridge: Connecting with Your Purpose

By Katherine Glass

Sit in a comfortable position. Breathing naturally, become aware of your heartbeat, centering yourself.

Visualize your tailbone, and imagine vibrant red light filling that area of the first chakra.

Breathe deeply in through your nose, inhale TRUST.
Exhale through your mouth, release FEAR.

Repeat three times.

Move the energy/awareness up to your abdomen area, the second chakra. Fill it with juicy bright orange light.

Inhale JOY, exhale APATHY. Repeat three times.

Move up to the solar plexus, the third chakra. Fill the area with bright golden yellow light. Breathe in CONFIDENCE, exhale DOUBT through your mouth.

Move the energy up into your heart, filling the heart chakra with emerald green or pink light. Deeply breathe in LOVE FOR ALL BEINGS, FOR YOURSELF, and exhale GRIEF.

Move up to the throat, the fifth chakra. Fill it with blue light. Inhale CLARITY, TRUTH. Exhale CONFUSION, FALSE EGO.

Now, bring the energy into your forehead, the brow chakra. Fill it with beautiful indigo. Inhale SPIRITUAL ECSTASY, exhale SEPARATENESS.

Moving up to the top of your head, the crown chakra, filling it up with glorious golden white light. Breathe in CONNECTION TO SOURCE, THE DIVINE, exhale FEAR and LONLINESS.

Expand the energy 360' around you, out as far as you can perceive. Bask in the Light of your Spirit, connected to
ALL BEINGS IN THE UNIVERSE.

"I am the rainbow bridge between Heaven and Earth in human form. I am eternal spirit. I am connected with Source, Creator, ALWAYS. Please put me in Your service today and every day of my life, for my highest purpose, and the Highest good. And so it is!"

Open your eyes, smile with gratitude for your gift of life, and share your LIGHT out in the world! We need you!

37

Sand Angels
By Karen S. Itin

Take a seat on the shoreline in the warm sand. Close your eyes, relax your breathing and concentrate on how your hands feel in the grains of sand. Feel at peace, and begin to move your hands back and forth at your sides in a slow, soft motion. Continue doing this slowly as the sand sifts between your fingers. Then, notice your feet, as you slide your toes into the sand and feel the coolness on your toes. Now, think about the tiny grains of sand covering your toes and how it feels against your skin. Sift the sand in your fingers as you run your fingers back and forth beside you. Listen to the refreshing water and breathe in each time the water hits the shore.

Release from your mind any unwanted thoughts and let the wave take it out to sea. Now fill up with the thought of each grain of sand sharing a blessing for you. Each grain of sand reads something like, "I belong to this vast beautiful world, and I am right where I need to be."

Another blessing would mention how you glow for your God, and how you share that bright light. Imagine how abundantly full your heart would feel if every positive blessing you have ever wished for would be said to you here, in these grains of sand.

With the sand filling you up, and the water washing your cares away, notice how peacefully refreshed you feel. Take a deep breath, blow out through your mouth, and begin to open your eyes.
Repeat the breathing twice more.

Peacefully begin your day, feeling refreshed and full of good blessings. And, look back, for your imprint that you made in the sand.

38

Equilibrium

By Kimber Bowers

Find an open space where you can stand comfortably. Inside or outside, anywhere that you like.

Inhale and exhale, surrendering any tension or negativity on the release of breath.

Continue to breathe in light and goodness at a steady pace, bringing your awareness to your surroundings, without discernment.

Notice the colors, the temperature, the light, the movement of the air against your skin. Notice any aromas, any tastes. Notice any sounds and the rhythm they carry. Feel the movement of your breath, noticing the air as it travels through your body, expanding and contracting. Take in the data of your senses. Be present in the sensuous experience of the moment, expanding the realization of all that IS.

Take a deep breath, bringing your arms up to the sky as you inhale.

Exhale, planting your feet firmly on the ground.

Allow the palms of your hands to connect to the energy of Spirit, while the soles of your feet become rooted in the energy of Earth. Feel this connection. Allow this balance. Sink into the feeling of harmony.

Know that this peace is within you, always. You are an infinite spirit in a physical existence, able to take in Divine Inspiration and embody it confidently on this earth. You are a beautiful expression of the One Divinity. Always connected. Love is ALWAYS available.

You are whole. You are connected. You are enough. Allow this realization to expand within you. Feel your heart open to receive transcendental love and to flow in alignment.

Gather the energy of heaven and earth, drawing it into your heart.

"I am walking in harmony with Spirit. Always connected. Always in Love."

Carry this affirmation with you throughout the day, and use it to re-establish a sense of peace and connection.

39

Invigorating Meditation and Visualization of Your Dream Home

By Mandy Berlin

Sit comfortably with your feet flat on the floor,
as we begin with a new breathing technique.
On your first try, simply stop when you have reached 15 seconds.

Begin to inhale and exhale rapidly through your nose, keeping your
mouth closed. Your breaths should be short and equal in length.
Attempt to inhale and exhale three times in one second.

(Each day, increase your time by five seconds, until you reach one
minute. Continue for a total of only 15 seconds your first time.)

Notice how revitalized you feel! Do this meditation whenever you wish
to elevate your energy level.

Now, with heightened awareness, begin to visualize the dream home that
you want to manifest in your life. Think about the home you have always
wanted. Now "see" it in your mind's eye. You feel great thinking about it
because it's your dream home!

Visualize getting out of your car and walking toward your new home.
What does it look like? Are there trees, grass, flowers? Desert landscape
around it? This is your home, and you can have whatever you want,
inside and out. Focus on the joy, the love, the beauty! You appreciate the
structure and ambience of your new environment.

How do the windows look? What do you see at your front door? Feel the
sturdy furniture that you and your loved ones/movers carry into your
home. These are the furnishings you have always wanted! As you enter
your home, take a mental "excursion" into each room. Imagine the walls,

curtains, blinds, floors; the layout of each room. You are grateful for your new surroundings and those who have assisted you today!

Keep personalizing it. See yourself decorating your home as you wish. Feel your ownership. After all, this is your dream home!

40

Activation for the
New Consciousness Rising

By Julie Geigle

Breathing deeply, open your heart to receive this beautiful activation.

Imagine expanding, evolving and ascending as this new energy on the planet supports you in all that you are, and all that you desire to become.

Allow this energy to raise you up to whatever level you desire. Trust and know that the Divine source energy, your angels and guides are always here to meet you where you are, and to bring you into that which you desire.

Your Spiritual Team never overwhelms; if things are moving too fast simply say ... slow down.

Now I want you to imagine a gauge within your mind. A gauge that you have total control over. This gauge you can turn up if you wish to experience more, turn down to experience less, or simply fine-tune like a radio dial tuning into your favorite station.

Fine tune this gauge now, adjusting it to the perfect level; the perfect station for you.

This small action will allow your transition, your adjustment to this new consciousness to be seamless, easy, effortless.

Imagine any struggles in your life dissolving, challenges disappearing.

You are now free, becoming one with your fullest potential, opening to all that you are and all that you came here to be.

Look upwards with your eyes closed and imagine a portal of communication opening, enabling a deeper and stronger connection to all that you desire. This portal is a link … linking up to your Spiritual Team.

Now, feel that beautiful wave of energy moving down through your entire being, feeling love and joy, peace and harmony. Moving that energy down through the bottom of your feet into planet earth, allowing all of the planet to receive these beautiful, sacred blessings of wealth, health, love and joy for all.

And so it is.

41

Good Morning Sunshine

By Marion Andrews

We begin by sitting in an upright, yet comfortable position,
back straight, spine aligned.

Taking a deep breath, slowly breathe in the morning,
breathe out the night.

Take a few more deep breaths, in through the nose
and slowly out through the mouth.

Settle into yourself.

Imagine the sun beaming down on you.

Feel the warmth of its rays welcoming you,
enfolding you in its radiant embrace.

Breathe in those rays.

Feel the warmth on the top of your head, not beating down so hot, but
surrounding you with the healthy glow from the Universe.

Now, let that warming beam flow into your crown chakra. Feel its energy
flowing down through your body, awakening each part of you as it
envelopes you in pleasant heat. It awakens each and every cell, until you
are glowing from the top of your head to the bottom of your feet, filling
you with the glorious, tender embrace from God,
the Source, the Universe.

Enjoy the embrace. Hold that feeling throughout your body, every cell
absorbing the healing light. Tingling. Mmmm, so comforting.

Feel the angels putting their wings around you. Softly folding you into the Universe's divine embrace. You are being held in this presence. Breathe it in. Your aura mingling with the Spirit-aura.

Stay aware of this glorious radiance. Love pouring over your entire being. Lighting your Body. Lighting your Mind. Lighting and loving your Spirit. Stay in this light and love.

Stay here. Stay here. Stay here.

Now, when you are ready, slowly come back to your reality. Breathe normally. Wiggle your toes and fingers, stretch like a cat, unwinding each vertebra, allowing your arms to move slowly, curl your shoulders. Delight in the afterglow.

You are glowing, filled with light. A beautiful start to your day.

42

Show Me My Purpose
By Karen Paolino Correia

Use Me for a Purpose Greater than I Know Myself.

I call upon Spirit, my angels, guides, masters and teachers, to surround me in a beautiful circle of love, light, healing, peace, and protection. Relax and imagine breathing as one with this unconditional love that surrounds us.
You know me better than I know myself, and therefore, I ask for your support and guidance. My deepest desire is to be in alignment to my highest potential, and to serve a purpose greater than I know myself. I trust that you, the divine, and my soul, knows exactly what this purpose is.

I choose to let go as I move my awareness from my thoughts in my head, where my ego would try to figure everything out, and I focus my attention in my heart (place your hand on your heart) where I can rest in the knowing that I will be shown and guided by the divine, every step of the way. Take a couple deep breaths in, and as you exhale, feel yourself letting go and focusing on the stillness in your heart.

I affirm this prayer from my heart: God use me for a purpose greater than I know myself, today and every day.

I ask that you guide me in a profound way to know how I may fulfill your purpose throughout my day; at home, at work, and with all those I encounter. I will remain open and I will pay attention as I listen to my intuition. I ask for your undeniable signs and synchronicities to support me and to show me the way to serve your purpose, greater than I know myself. I also ask that you provide me with the knowing and the courage to take inspired action when I am guided to do so.

43

Snow Flake
By Catherine Madeira

There is a spirit whose unnoticed numbers are so colossal, reaching past the grains of sand; far exceeding the infinite number of stars in our Galaxy. Those found on Earth alone, if contemplated, would dwarf the imagination of the God essence itself.

Alone, it's a small, silent, delicate, vulnerable short-lived entity; meeting its demise in even the slightest disturbance.

But as its infinite numbers mount—joining together, building as one—so does its potential power and fury, demanding submission and respect.

It may choose to grant beautiful silent safe passage, or on its whim, thunder down in deadly unescapable dominance.

THE SNOW FLAKE.

Through four billion years, how many single snowflakes have fallen? Each featherlight, blanketing time and time again the Mother Gaia, allowing her a cool slumber as she builds strength to parent so lovingly spring's excited awakening.

44

Dreamcatcher
By Liana Salas

Today is a new day. Starting now, I go from being a dream chaser,
to a Dreamcatcher.

Today, I dream with my eyes open. I take time to visualize myself living
my greatest dreams. I decide what is possible and dream without limits.
Happiness, health, abundance, joy and love are all part of my dream.

I know there is a power greater than me that supports me
unconditionally. I trust my dreams will become my reality in perfect
timing. I know that there are lessons to learn along the journey to my
dreams. I am not waiting until my dreams come true to be happy.
I choose to be happy on my way to my dreams.

Today, I smile more often. I keep my heart open. I choose thoughts and
actions that nourish my body. I love and appreciate my body, because my
body allows me to live my dreams.

No matter what today brings, I believe in myself and my ability to
achieve my dreams. I keep moving forward and taking actions that align
with my dreams, and bring me closer to where I want to be. I move
through my day with faith. I keep my dreams in my mind, feel them in
my heart, and believe with certainty that miracles will
manifest in my life.

Today is a new day, and I am one step closer to catching all my dreams.

45

Blessed Hands
By Charmaine Gagnon

Sit quietly with your hands open, resting gently in your lap.

Breathe deeply, and focus on your hands.

Study your hands with awe and wonder.

Think about how your hands have served you.

How many times have these hands brought food and drink to your lips, to nourish you?

How many times have these hands prepared a meal for you or another?

How many times have these hands held a book that nourished your soul?

How many times have these hands touched the fabric of the clothing you chose to wear, reaching to select an item from a closet or drawer?

How many times have these hands gently washed your face and all of your body?

How many times have these hands smoothed your hair as you brushed it?

How many times have these hands caressed the face of a loved one, or someone in need?

How many times have these hands brushed a tear from your cheek or someone else's?

How many times have these hands held the hands of another?

How many times have these hands held a newborn baby?

How many times have these hands touched a kitten or a puppy
or a bunny?

How many times have these hands held a card or letter from a loved one?

Your hands are a beautiful blessed part of your body, and a beautiful part
of your history.

Close your eyes and think of other ways that your hands
have served you.

Then gently bring your hands to your heart and give thanks for the way
your hands have blessed your life.

Breathe deeply and feel the gratitude.

Set an intention for how your hands will serve you today.

Have a beautiful, blessed day!

46

Morning Meditation to
Be One with Nature

By Vicki Snyder-Young

As I wake up this beautiful morning, I take a deep breath and inhale all
that is good in my world. I exhale the drowsiness from my night's sleep.
I settle into a steady calming breath.

I envision I am in a relaxed and peaceful place in nature. Today it may be
a forest, a meadow, stream or a favorite childhood place. I close my eyes
and let my imagination run free. I immerse myself in the environment as
if we were one. I glimpse the blue sky with puffy clouds. I perceive the
trees, plants and all the beings that live here, from the furry ones to the
insects. I know I am safe and secure.

I smell the pine trees, grasses, flowers and the sweet air.
Their smells comfort and ground me.

I listen to the sounds that dance around me. I hear a deer pass as he steps
on the drying leaves; they crinkle under his foot. The birds sing as they
take flight; the crickets chirp. I hear the messages they bring. They are
telling me to quiet my mind, listen and be one with them.

I feel the stillness; it encircles me, and I am at ease. I feel the warm sun
and breeze hit my face. I smile for it is heavenly sitting here, allowing
my senses to take in all nature has to say. I can feel the heartbeat of
Mother Earth; we are in perfect rhythm. I have no other cares right now.
I just delve into the feelings and messages the universe provides
me at this moment.

As I sit, I offer prayers and ask for guidance. I take time to receive the
messages from the universe.

I start my day with gratitude and marvel in the magic of nature.

47

All Is Well

By Cynthia Stoneman

As I wake, it is still dark outside and my body is heavy.

All will be well.

I stretch my arms ... legs ... and back, as my body starts to move.

When my feet touch the floor, my mind starts the list of things to do today. I write them down and quiet my mind.

All will be well.

The bathroom light is bright and my eyes squeeze shut. I breathe slowly and deeply ... grounding myself.

I visualize the events on my daily list as completed with grace and ease. There is joy and fun in everything to be done.

There are helpful people everywhere.
I am grateful and receptive for their assistance.

All will be well.

It is a beautiful day. I am healthy and happy. I am present in each moment. I see the silver lining in all challenges. Today is an adventure and I intend to enjoy it.

All will be well.

Doors are opened for me today. Smiles and kind words surround me. I am fully supported in everything I do. I give and accept kindness easily. I am energetic and at peace. I feel love all around me.

All is well.

48

I Am the Love & Light
By Kelli Adkins

With my feet firmly on the ground and my eyes closed, I see strong, healthy root-like structures shoot from my feet to the center of the earth. These roots wrap around the core of the earth many times over. In doing so, I am firmly grounded and stabilized, no matter what comes at me throughout my day.

Through these healthy roots, I feel warm golden energy from the earth's center. It rises up through the roots to touch my feet. The warm golden energy enters my feet and travels up through my legs. It works its way up to the hips, torso and chest. The healing light warms and heals every cell it touches. The light continues up and down my arms and shoots out from my fingertips. It then moves its way back to my neck and head. This loving energy flows from the center of the earth, touching and healing every cell along the way, providing energy, love and light. The light finally shoots from the top of my head, straight up to heaven. I am a clear vessel of love and light.

I release busyness.

I let go of the fear of boredom.

I let go of perfection.

I choose peace.

I am okay with being still.

I embrace the quiet.

I allow things to unfold as they are supposed to.

Clarity comes to me in stillness.

Self-care is an act of self-love.

Self-care is not selfish.

Self-care allows me to be present and more able to shine my light for others.

I love myself as I love others.

I love myself as He loves me.

I release all that is not serving me to allow room for what does.

I am the love and light so desperately needed in the world today.

49

Today's Your Day
By Cheryl Carrigan

Place your hand on your heart ... still yourself ... feel your heart beat ...
focus inward, feel your soul.

Today is a new day ... a day waiting just for you … inhale ... to step out
into the world, like you have never done before.

Today we are going to be open ... raw, naked, no mask, no hiding …

Just the unbelievable, beautiful soul that you truly are …
yet you hide from this world.

As you step out ... feel the love, feel the cheers, feel the joy … coming
from those around you who have waited so long for your true arrival.

Your day has come ... today is your day.

You can never turn back, for now they know who you really are ... and it
is enough … all is well ... all is well.

Stand tall ... breathe in ... today you see the real world, and the special
beauty of it is, the world gets to see the real you.

50

Journey to Self-Love
By Tina Palmer

In order to bond with anyone else, we need to develop a bond of love with ourselves that often gets lost in our adulthood.

Find a comfortable place to relax, soften your eyes, and take a few long cleansing breaths. Do this several times if needed to get to that relaxed state. Allow any tension in you to melt away.

Imagine above yourself is a beautiful, warm, gold, healing light; and allow that light to penetrate throughout your entire body, as if you are pouring this light in through the crown of your head.

Now picture a younger version of yourself standing before you. Reach out to that child in whatever way feels best, and ask if you can spend some time together.

Visualize that golden light growing and expanding all around you both. See yourself wrapping this child in the light so that you two become one big ball of light together.

If this brings up some painful feelings, embrace them. This is the time to pour on self-love.

Inside this bubble of light, tell this beautiful innocent child that you are loved, you are accepted, and you are safe.

Promise this child that you will always be there to protect and nurture them. Lock eyes with this child in front of you and smile.

Understand that all that has happened in your life has brought you to the miracle you are today.

Breathe in the beauty of this child before you. Breathe in the love, the acceptance, and the compassion. Visualize this child growing into the adult you are today.

Visualize this glorious glow of light radiating brighter and stronger between you. Breathe into appreciation the love that you are.

When you are ready, gently bring your awareness back to your body and open your eyes.

51

May I Remember Who I AM
By Linda Lee

Breathe deeply and relax. Read this morning meditation slowly. Sit quietly and reflect on whatever arises for you. Journal with the intention to engage your day with conscious compassion, for yourself and others.

May I Remember Who I AM.

May I remember to explore fearlessness.

May I remember to wander more freely in my wild, inner landscape.

May I remember that each encounter is a holy one.

May I remember to sit in full presence with the other.

May I remember to replace judgement with curiosity and understanding.

May I remember to be a holy cup of tea to the broken-hearted.

May I remember to diminish no one.

May I remember to seek and give forgiveness.

May I remember to be a safe harbor for the lonely,
the frightened and the searching.

May I remember to allow myself to surrender to Divine Guidance.

May I remember to welcome the intimacy of Divine Presence
into my heart.

May I remember to be open to asking and receiving.

May I remember to radiate light and goodness to the world.

May I remember to embrace the oneness of that world.

May I remember who I AM today.

52

Awakening the Sexy Gorgeous Soul Within

By April-Anjali McCray

You may sit or stand comfortably.

Cover your eyes gently, laying your fingers sideways over each eye.

Take in a deep breath, and as you release your breath, slide your fingers to your temples as you repeat:

"I awaken the divine light within me."

Slide your fingers up and over your ears and down your neck resting upon your shoulders and affirm:

"I awaken with magic in my mind and choose only the thoughts that bring peace to my soul."

Leaving your arms in place, simply cross over your hands to each opposite shoulder, resting your hands in a loving embrace on each arm and affirm:

"It is my goddess given right to be truly supported and loved in this life."

Breathe in deeply, and as you exhale, smooth your hands down the arms with a featherlight touch, and as your hands meet, rest them on your solar plexus and affirm:

"I am overflowing with goddess wisdom, beauty and vitality."

"I AM enough in all ways in my life."

Slide your hands from your solar plexus down the front of your body and down your legs and sweep your hands off the top of your feet.

Then bring your hands up in an energetic sweeping motion straight back up your body and sweep over your breasts and land at your face. As you cradle your cheeks in your hands affirm:

"I am endless, timeless and eternal."

And take a deep breath in, push your arms straight above your head and as you float your arms down like a radiant sunburst affirm:

"Joy comes in no greater form of expression than when it flows freely from the richness of my sexy gorgeous soul."

And end with deep affirming breath and a sexy gorgeous smile.

53

Radiating Love Through Your Heart's Golden Spiral

By Lisa A. Clayton

Focus your attention on the area around your heart.
Breathe into your heart area deeper and slower than normal.
Continue to focus on heart breathing for 1-2 minutes.

Now, with each breath, activate the feeling of appreciation, love and care
for someone or something in your life.
Feel this appreciation, love and care fill your heart completely.

Next, imagine a golden spiral is glowing in your heart.
With each breath, visualize giving movement and liveliness
to your golden spiral.

Feel your golden spiral expanding with its movement,
filling your heart completely.
As it moves, it may be inside or outside your heart area.
Imagine it going either horizontally or vertically through your body as it
expands fully with each breath.

Let the expansiveness and movement of your heart's golden spiral
sweep away all fear, doubts and worries.
Feel its golden light and sparkle dissolving negative feelings,
unforgiveness, anxiety or stress.

This golden spiral represents your heart's essence that is uniquely yours;
guiding you to feel greater love, care and appreciation
for yourself and others.
Keep breathing into your golden spiral and honor its unique loveliness.

Take deeper breaths into your golden spiral to feel it gain strength and acceleration.
Imagine it pumping golden liquid throughout your body in each vein, artery and capillary.
Feel the luminous, golden liquid saturating every cell.
With each breath, visualize golden rays of love beaming brilliantly within you and outside your body.

Just as your physical heart beats to keep you alive, your golden heart spiral is your spiritual heart beat signaling to Source, your Angels and Spiritual Guides.
Your heart's golden radiance serves as a beacon to invite communion and connection with ALL for higher, Divine love.

As you move and rest throughout your day, activate your golden spiral for radiating your heart's love.

54

Heartful Communication
By Julie Ann Marie

Find a comfortable position. Take three deep breaths in through your nose, and out through your mouth. As you inhale, expand your openness to receive. As you exhale, thank and release any mind chatter.

From this place of openness, focus in on your heart. Feel its smooth and steady beat. Notice how it responds as you breathe in and out, and how breath and beat synchronize. While merging into this balance, tune in to your blood. Feel it pulsing in and out of your heart.

Look at your blood. Feel into its oxygen rich, red cells. Travel with these cells through your vessels as they deliver nurturing sustenance to every cell in your body. This happens every moment of the day, whether you are awake or asleep. What is the message that these cells carry? Take some time to talk with them. Ask them how they feel; is their structure and movement easy, smooth, and effortless? Are they feeling sluggish? Or something in-between?

From this place, thank them for sharing. Ask them if there is anything they need. Your cells are always listening and ready to share their wisdom.

As it returns to the heart, notice your blood releasing what it no longer needs. It works efficiently with all of your organs to co-create optimal health.

Thank your blood for the life force energy it provides to sustain your body. As you do this, observe what happens. Do the cells smile? Do they expand and grow? Notice the power of your thought and the speed with which energy shifts. Spend some time basking in this mutual loving connection.

Know that your body is your best friend, and is always working to achieve your best health. Sense, feel, experience and embrace the miracle that is you!

55

Guardian Angel Meditation:
A Guided Meditation
By Sunny Dawn Johnston

Visualize a rich, vibrant, colorful room. This room is like nothing you've seen before. As you enter, you begin to feel an amazing sense of calm and quiet. Once inside, you are greeted by a beautiful spiral staircase that leads upstairs. Begin walking up the staircase, one step at a time, until you reach the top.

Once at the top, you notice that you have drifted to a new place. This place is your most exquisite place on earth. Notice where you are. Is there sand at your feet? Are you standing in a flower-filled garden? Are you frolicking in the ocean? Take a minute and feel the peace that fills your heart. Notice if there are any scents. Can you hear the sounds? Take a moment to experience this place that your Spirit is guiding you to. Feel it … embrace it.

And now, you see a gorgeous bright light and you know that it is time to meet your Guardian Angel. Appearing right before you is your resplendent, loving, gentle Guardian Angel. You can feel the unconditional loving energy of your Guardian Angel as you meet him/her for the very first time. Get to know your Guardian Angel. What is his/her name? What messages might he/she have for you? Take the next few minutes to listen to the guidance that your Guardian Angel has for you.

Finally, share with your Guardian Angel how very glad you are to have had this time together. It is now time to leave this special place. Thank your Guardian Angel as you turn to leave. As you walk back, you'll find yourself in the rich, vibrant, colorful room where you began; feeling and knowing that your Guardian Angel is truly always by your side.

56

Meditation to Embody Divine Radiance
By Bobbe Bramson

Letting your eyes softly close, take these next several moments to go on a journey within. Attune to the gentle in and out of your breathing, so dependable in each arising moment of now, and now, and now. Simply allow the breath's perfect rhythm to guide you into a place of quiet repose ...

Here in this sacred space you can choose to make conscious contact with your Inner Radiance. It is the part of you that is pure love, that is indestructible, eternal, and in complete resonance with the Divine.

Sense yourself surrounded by a golden orb of protective Light and Love. Surrender into its healing, soothing warmth and feel how every cell, every molecule becomes infused with shimmering rays of Light. Your entire energy field is lit from within and pulsates with golden Light.

Notice how the luminous glow of your Inner Radiance begins to harmonize and blend with Divine Radiance until your heart and the Cosmic Heart beat as one ...

Tension melts away as you relax into the tender embrace of deep peace and serenity. You know that you are loved and accepted unconditionally for who you are, as you are, right now.

Shimmering Divine energy flows into your mind, cleansing it of any doubt, fear, or self-perceived limitation until your mind is clear and blessedly still. Take a moment now to rest in this golden clarity and quiet ...

Feel as rays of Pure Radiance extend from your heart and permeate your entire being, filling you with joy, hope, freedom, imperturbability and strength ...

When you are ready, come back into the grounded here and now, fully present and aware, trusting that the Light, Love, and healing shifts have been anchored firmly within you.

57

Morning Chakra Balance Meditation with Crystals and the Archangels

By Skye Angelheart

Lying on a table fashioned out of glittering smoky quartz, in a soothing forest of amethyst, you are immersed in the relaxing, healing energy of crystals and the Archangels. They are surrounding you in love, ready to be of service.

Gabriel approaches you and lays a red jasper crystal upon your root chakra, at the base of your spine, grounding your energy and enabling you to feel safe and secure at all times.

Haniel then leans over you and gently places a piece of moonstone upon your sacral chakra, located below your navel. The moonstone supports you in releasing emotions that no longer serve your highest good, allowing you to be present.

Uriel comes forward and sets an amber stone upon your solar plexus chakra, situated above your navel. The amber ignites your flame of self-empowerment, and the fire burns brightly as you fully embrace your power.

Ariel softly moves forward and places a gorgeous heart-shaped stone of rose quartz onto your heart chakra, bathing your heart in unconditional love, compassion and acceptance.

Raguel takes his place at your neck and sets a sparkling stone of aquamarine on your throat chakra, infusing all of your communications with truth and integrity as you confidently express yourself with love.

Chamuel appears at your side, placing a fluorite crystal upon your third eye chakra, located between your brows. The fluorite gently opens your third eye, enabling you to view all of your experiences with clarity.

Jeremial now situates himself at your crown chakra, placing a twinkling stone of amethyst upon it, strengthening your connection to your higher self and the divine.

As you breathe in deeply, a rainbow of light travels throughout your chakras, activating, cleansing and balancing them as you prepare to begin this beautiful day with intention.

Note: This meditation may be used with or without the physical application of crystals.

58

Meditation to Connect to Source
By Giuliana Melo

Begin by placing a hand on your heart and connect with your breath. Breathe in deeply and mindfully. Exhale and relax your body.

Imagine white light coming in through your crown chakra at the top of your head. Allow it to run through your body, out the bottom of your feet and deep into Mother Earth, to anchor and ground you. Then, imagine it flowing all the way up again and out through your heart chakra, until you visualize yourself surrounded in a bubble of white light.

Affirm: I am a child of the light. I have within me deep wisdom and knowledge to carry me through this day with ease and Grace. I am a powerful co-creator with Source. I can manifest all my dreams. I am love. I am safe. I am Divinely supported at all times.
Thank you, and so it is.

59

Tree of Life – Connecting and Grounding with Nature

By Julie Gale

Sit or stand, preferably next to a tree of your choice. Barefoot is best, so kick off those shoes! Stand in a position where you can move freely.

Slowly raise your arms out to your sides until they are parallel with your shoulders.

Slowly breathe in and out … feel the breath filling your heart.

Look to the sky as you raise your arms slowly until both of your hands meet over your head, palms touching.

Now, bring your joined hands down towards your chest, as you focus on the radiance of this energy spreading through your body. Rest your hands at your heart chakra.

Say out loud or in your head:

"I am one with the energy of the earth. I am one with those who walk with me. I am one.

I feel one with the energy of the earth. I feel strength move within me. I feel the life force flow through the soles of my feet."

Breathe in the power of the earth.

Now, move your hands (still with palms together) straight upwards, over your head and extend your arms out, like you are forming the shape of the canopy of the tree, and stop them once they are parallel with your shoulders.

Say out loud or in your head:

"Today I will speak peace and seek well-being for the highest good for all inhabitants of the planet. My heart trusts and will not be shaken. I will act compassionately toward all and see the beauty all around me."

Now move your hands and arms down to your sides.

Take another deep breath in and out.

With one hand touching the tree and your feet firmly on the earth, say: "Namasté".

Now, walk with nature and stay grounded throughout your day.

60

Activate Abundance with the Angels and Fairies

By Courtney Long

Get comfortable, close your eyes, and breathe deeply.

With each inhale, breathe in love. With each exhale, release fear.

Place your hands on your heart and imagine a gorgeous, radiant light glowing in your heart-space. This is your inner light of abundance. Allow the light to glow brighter, filling your body, expanding beyond your body, and forming a cocoon of light around you.

Notice how the vibration of abundance feels. Affirm silently or aloud, "I am an abundant being living in an abundant universe. Abundance is my divine birthright, and I lovingly claim it now! The more I receive, the more I give. The more I give, the more I receive. The Universe abundantly supports us all!"

Next, call on the Angels and Fairies by saying, "Good morning, Angels and Fairies of Abundance! Thank you for your presence. I am open and ready to activate abundance in my life."

Set an intention for a specific form of abundance you wish to experience today, whether an abundance of love, romance, joy, fulfillment, money (if so, declare a specific amount and what you will use the money for), opportunities to help others, divine guidance, or anything else your soul desires.

Say to the Angels and Fairies, "Today I choose to experience _____ (fill in the blank with your intention). Thank you for helping me manifest this or something even better, aligned with the highest good. I am open to magic and miracles. I am grateful and excited about all the abundance that flows in my life! Thank you, and so it is!"

Spend a few moments in silence, imagining yourself enjoying abundance. Also, be open to receiving guidance from the Angels and Fairies.

Finally, anchor in the abundance by celebrating, such as singing, dancing or stretching your arms and opening your heart.

61

Begin Your Day Feeling Centered, Present, Grounded and Strong

By Micara Link

Good Morning, please take a moment to find a comfortable position for your body to be in for a few minutes.

Once settled, begin to look around the room. Even if you've been in this room hundreds of times, look around and notice the different colors, textures, shapes and varying levels of light ... taking it in as if it's the first time your eyes have seen it.

When you feel complete, lower your eyes or close your eyes completely, turning your awareness inward.

Notice how your body feels this morning. Become aware of the sensations throughout your body ... notice any areas that feel tight, constricted or held ... and notice areas that feel open, light and expansive. Check in with yourself from a place of curiosity and compassion, letting go of any desire to control, fix or judge.

Be with yourself just as you are today.

Sense into your whole body ... from the top of your head to the tips of your toes. Holding your whole body in your awareness.
Feel your presence here.

Feel your breath. Your beautiful, effortless breath ...

Right here. Right now.

Breathing into your day.

Locate a place somewhere in your body where you sense your center.

When you locate it, if you're able, rest your hand there.

Begin to breathe into this space ... feel your center ... feel your body here, grounded and strong ...

Sense how this space expands with each breath ... feeling supported, safe, and secure with each inhale and exhale.

Get really acquainted with this space. Sense into it from all directions and notice if it has a shape, size, texture or color.

This is your center. Your place of strength, power and resiliency.

Spend a few minutes here. When you're ready, slowly open your eyes to begin your day feeling grounded, centered, present and strong.

62

Field of Sunflowers
By Lori Kilgour Martin

Angel greetings on this new morning. With your permission, Archangel Ariel would like to lead you to a quiet, mystical sanctuary. This path you walk on together is an ancient one.

When you arrive, notice the open field and a soft place to sit. Sunflowers tall, form a circle all around you. There is a large quartz crystal shimmering in the ground below. As you begin to breathe, with your inner vision, see this sacred space filling up with the colors of soft pink, lavender and gold. So beautiful, you are held in an etheric cocoon.

Small butterflies, iridescent blue ones, have arrived. With your permission, they will lift away threads of energy that are no longer needed from your body, taking them up and up on a ribbon of rainbow light. They are guiding you to the area or memory in need of releasing, which may benefit you the most this morning. It might be a recent one, or one from long ago.

During this time, a re-calibration is taking place. Gentle, this process is dancing at the cellular level, as well as around your aura, your light body. The swirling motion is both healing and nurturing, beginning with your heart and expanding outward. God is blessing you with abiding faith. Archangel Ariel shares: *Breathe, relax as you are able and know you are safe and loved beyond measure.*

The sun is rising now, its hues begin to radiate fully in this peaceful sanctuary. Its deep orange glow is inviting you to slowly bring your awareness back. Feel the divine warmth flow, which will carry you through the day. The Christ within shines brightly. Allow your heart to open up even more to receive another message: *All is well.*

63

Today I Rise

By April L. Dodd, M.A.

I'm Alive!

What a blessed gift I have been given to rise newly!

To rise above,
To rise beyond,
To rise as the Truth of Life Itself.
Right here, right now,
Surrendering only to the wellspring of Newness
That pulses within me
With every breath of my aliveness.

Every interaction,
Everything I do,
Everyone I meet,
Or even think about today,
May they be fed from it.

May I encase myself in this newness
And see it, know it, appreciate it in all others.
For newness is the way.
Without it, I am old.
With it, I am everything.

Today I rise, embraced by the All,
Ever-expanding as I allow it.
Held by wonder, always stalking the mystery:
I am.

Today I rise as the divine being that I am,
Using my human experience to create possibilities
That enhance everything and disturbs nothing.

Today I rise as the extraordinary being that I am,
Consciously participating with this pulse of aliveness,
Following its lead wherever I go and with whom I come in contact,
Knowing that I am the evidence of spirit finding it's
Celebration through me!

Alive in this Truth,
Amen.

64

Hermosa

By Jennifer Ross

Lay back, close your eyes, relax your mind and body.

Visualize Hermosa Beach: the serenity, the love, and the
beauty of the ocean.

Find calm within your soul; take a deep breath in and out.

Spread the gentle calm to the rest of your being.

Breathe in the calm slowly and deeply.

Breathe out any concerns.

Feel and breathe in the wild ocean air as the waves spill over, and gently
splash at your feet.

Absorb the sensation from the Hermosa ocean waves until they bring you
to a calm tranquility.

Be the grounded one with the soft sands of the earth against you.

Let any thoughts that come in flow gently through your being
and exit effortlessly.

Gently wrap your fingers around the ocean treasure that has flowed into
your palm and bring it close to your soul, while paying close attention
to your breathing...

Explore the exquisite seashell with your fingertips; allow it to remind
you of the life, love and freedom you have been yearning for.

Feel that ocean treasure as it releases love and life into your being, ever so gently.

Hold your breathing steady; this will allow the freedom in your soul to awaken.

Realize that the freedom of choice is yours.

It's in your possession...

Be who you want to be.

Authored in Hermosa Beach, California, USA

65

This Day

By Susan Barrett

I start this day with gratitude for all those around me.

I start this day with gratitude for all those I will be interacting with today.

I start this day with peace for all those I come in contact with.

I start this day with the hope of world peace in my heart.

I start this day with compassion for those suffering.

I start this day with compassion for all hardship.

I live this day with love and grace.

66

A Journey Inward
By Katrina L. Wright

Preparation:

Choose a comfortable place to meditate. When you meditate in one place regularly, it is easier to move right into the meditation vibration that you've established there. Your meditation space is the doorway to your inner-world. The more sacred you can make it, the better. Use a peaceful timer (you can download one for your phone), and set it for 20 minutes.

Meditation:

With softly closed eyelids and relaxed arms and shoulders, cup your hands, one hand underneath the other. Feel the weight of your body as it is completely supported by a chair or the floor. Take three deep, slow breaths in, while simply noticing how the air feels as it enters and is released. Next, count slowly as you inhale from 1 to 4. At the top of the inhale hold for 3 seconds. Then, on the exhale, slowly count from 1 to 6, and again hold for 3 seconds at the bottom of your exhale. Repeat 8-16 times. Next, silently repeat to yourself: "I do no-thing. I am no-thing. I enjoy being." Repeat this silently to yourself, integrating it with your natural breathing rhythm. Allow whatever feelings, emotions or expressions that emerge from within to simply be; it's okay to laugh, smile or cry. Become 'one' with your breath.
Do this until you hear your alarm.

Post Meditation:

Keeping your eyes closed, rub your hands together gently, roll your shoulders and rotate your head circularly; become aware of your surroundings. You may open your eyes whenever you are ready.

67

Today, in this Moment, I Honor Me
By Cris T Linn

Today, I honor the now. As I slide out of bed and my feet touch the floor, I sit tall, taking a deep breath. I allow Divine Love to flood through my body and fill my heart with gratitude for another day.

In this moment, the worries of my past and future no longer serve me. My joy is now, in this very moment. For I know, it is from this space that all else is created.

Today, I honor each breath as it flows through me. I breathe in Divine Order and exhale the chaos of my mind.

In this moment, as my mind shows me the plans for the day, I do not see obstacles; I clearly see the day flowing with ease and anticipate it all with joy.

Today, I will honor each emotion that surfaces with understanding instead of judgement.

In this moment, I feel the divine order of life when quieting my mind and listening to my heart. I give my heart permission to express its truth, and teach me to follow its guidance and lead the way.

Today, I honor my choices, realizing within each choice lies my destiny.

In this moment, with every sign, I receive validation that I am on my path.

Today, I honor my thoughts, remembering how influential they are to Divine creation.

In this moment, I dismiss each negative thought before it can define my path. I choose to create a brighter, more positive reality and acknowledge that this is where I begin to build the life I love.

Today, when I lie down in my bed, giving gratitude for all that was this day, I honor me.

In this moment, I know I've done the best can, and I am enough.

68

Morning Mindfulness
By Wayson Wight

Sit in a comfortable cross-legged position (head over heart, heart over pelvis), and use your breath to hold your attention.

Here are two great methods to begin a mindfulness practice:

1) Say the word "inhale" to yourself as you breathe in, then count on your exhale. I count to 10 and start over when I either reach 10, or my mind drifts off course. Rinse and Repeat.

2) Use visuals. Imagine a rising and cresting wave pattern that is synchronized with your breath. Use as much detail as possible and make an audible breath out. Imagine the sound of waves cresting on a beach. Remember, the goal here isn't perfection and uninterrupted attention.

The process of losing focus, going off on a train of thought, then returning to the breath is the exact skill we're trying to develop. Do not get discouraged. Simply acknowledge with kindness that you lost focus and return your attention to your breath. That's it! The process of failing is the lesson. Through practice, your ability to focus and monitor your thoughts will improve and you'll be in the driver's seat of your moment-to-moment experience. Cultivating this skill of watching your mind operate in its usual pattern can then be used to alter it to a healthier state of mind.

Here's an example: Imagine you're running late and you see stopped traffic on the interstate. An undisciplined mind may begin to panic and lead you down a path of what-if, worst case scenarios. In contrast, a skillful mind, with daily mindfulness practice, would catch the initial thoughts and set a healthier course. One might say, "This is out of my control and I'll get to work as soon as the situation allows. It's not the end of the world and my boss will understand."

69

Breath of Fresh Release
By Kia Abilay

Imagine gentle, swirling energy gracefully spiraling through your body from the top of your head, out the bottoms of your feet. Set the intention of release. Repeat several times.

Allow any sounds wanting expression … a sigh … a laugh … a tear … a groan ... a scream, as you traverse through your system experiencing a full liberation.

Clear out any other dust or cobwebs bringing you down ... you can identify them or let go without naming them. Feel free of the thoughts that clutter your mind.

Sweep the residue away with an energetic broom. Exhilarating breaths bring us to a place of solace.

A sweet fragrance of peppermint cleanses your system as you release the residue of thoughts lingering in your body and soul. Breathe in the freshness and relax.

Breathe in your favorite soothing fragrance, elevating your senses to clarity. Allow the love of the divine to penetrate your body and soul in peace and joy. Savor the stillness.

Your aura is filled with contentment. You have prepared for the company of universal blessings. Linger and relish in this tranquility. Throughout the day, recall the essence … inhale and exhale, creating a smile and a sigh of serenity.

70

I AM
By Kelli Lee Sappenfield

The statement "I AM" is one of the most powerful statements in all of creation, for what comes after it is what you are divinely declaring.
So today declare your truth.
Repeat out loud:

I AM.
I AM kind.
I AM friendly.
I AM peaceful.
I AM joyful.
I AM grateful.
I AM adventurous.
I AM fearless.
I AM spirit.
I AM energy.
I AM wealthy.
I AM beautiful.
I AM abundant.
I AM evolving.
I AM love.
I AM mystical.
I AM magical.
I AM vibration.
I AM fortunate.
I AM blessed.
I AM all-encompassing.
I AM divine.
I AM healthy.
I AM strong.
I AM powerful.
I AM empowered.

I AM funny.
I AM focused.
I AM successful.
I AM universal.
I AM connected.
I AM consciousness.
I AM special.
I AM worthy.
I AM happy.
I AM all and all is me!

71

Soul Infusion to Kick-Start Your Day
By Julie Gale

Try this meditation before you even get out of bed!

Begin with deep breaths, filling your heart, body, mind and soul with each breath. Feel each of the cells in your body tingle and expand.

Envision a glowing white light just above your head. The glowing white light is beaming, with light rays all around it. Slowly, the white light starts to flow through the crown of your head. The bright light fills the backs of your eyelids. Pause here for a moment in the light and say out loud or to yourself:

"Today, I put forth my intentions for the greatest good for all. I only have positive thoughts and will put my energy towards that which serves me best."

The white light continues to glow, moving past your chin, where it now pauses at your throat. Say out loud or to yourself:

"Today, I will only speak the voice of love."

The light moves through you and is now at your heart.
Your chest expands and is filled with divine love.
You are reminded that you are loved.

Now the white light, made from the same white light of which we are all born from, moves to your belly - your solar plexus. Your solar plexus glows with the divine light. You feel an awareness of always having love, food and all of life's necessities. You feel an abundance of prosperity. You send this out to the world now.

The white light is still moving, now through to your base, your root chakra. You are reminded that you are safe, protected, and provided for.

Finally, let the white light move down through your legs, into the soles of your feet. As you are wiggling your toes, imagine the white light flowing out into the Universe.

72

Seed of Creation
By Julie Ann Marie

With pen and paper, write down a question, intention or desire you would like insight and guidance on. Focusing inward, take three deep, grounding breaths. Inhale, grounding down through your feet, deep into Mother Earth. Exhale, connecting and anchoring your energy with the ever-present field of universal, Divine love consciousness.

In this unified field you have created, take a look around. Notice where your third eye is drawn to. Is it a place in your body, on the Earth or celestial? Is it another being, a spirit guide or other wisdom keeper? Or something else entirely? Whatever it is, know it is exactly right for you in this moment.

Keeping your third eye focused, open your hand to receive a seed being given to you. Notice it's feel, texture, weight, smell and energetic signature. Does it offer you a feeling, emotion, color, words or sound? This seed has heard your call and is ready for integration with your body, mind and spirit.

While in communion with this seed, plant it in your heart. Notice how your loving attention nurtures, waters and fertilizes it as it starts growing roots to become part of you. Do you notice any shifts in your body, mind or spirit? Breathe into these shifts, allowing them to deepen even more.

Turn your focus outward, towards the unified field of Divine love consciousness. Do you notice any changes in the field and your place in it? Thank the field for the gift of this seed. Know that it is always there, supporting you through life.

As you go about your day, periodically check in. Is what you are thinking, feeling or doing strengthening the seed? How do you feel different? Play with shifting your thoughts to see and know what helps it thrive.

73

Meditation to Begin Your Day Through Nurturing & Nourishing Yourself

By Gina Barbara

Start by making yourself comfortable, in a position most suitable for you,
with eyes closed or open …

Begin to take a few deep breaths, in through your nose
and out through your mouth.

Feel your breath rise up – in through your nose,
and out through your mouth.

Continue to breathe away,
while now shifting your awareness to your navel area.

Place your hands on your tummy. Feel the rise and fall
of the tummy with the breath.

Breathe in … feel it rise up …

Out … feel the fall …

Continue to feel the rise and fall as you breathe away.

And now, imagine a beautiful ball of golden/orange light
being offered into your tummy.

Feel the golden ray of light beneath your hands, as they continue
to move with the rise and fall.

Notice the expansion of your breath as you draw it in fully on the in
breath, and expand even more on the out breath.

Breathe … so that your vibration is pulsating larger than
your external body.

Feel the expansion and fullness of your being through your tummy.

And slowly pull that energy back within you, so that the breath you give out, returns to you … expanding your vibrational presence … in and out.

Gently return your awareness to your tummy, knowing that you are completely nourished and replenished.

You're ready to start your day, knowing you have greater connection to your natural flow.

Allow yourself to move through your day,
coming back to this rhythm at any time …

Know you are completely supported, nourished and replenished in your mind, body and spirit …

And on an out breath, start your day with presence!

74

Heart of Community

By Ellen Elizabeth Jones

May I be a friend to those without friendship.

A luminary for those who journey.

A life boat, a bridge, a pathway

For those seeking expansion.

May the hurt of every living creature

Be transmuted in divine love.

May I be the conduit of healing, and the medicine,

And may I be the caregiver

For all the wounded beings in the world,

Until all are well.

Just like the stars in the heavens

And of the vast matter in Earth,

May I always respect the life

Of all the unbridled creatures.

And until they transcend from affliction

May I also be the source of JOY,

For ALL, in every realm, and in all time and space.

May this prayer and its power last forever.

And So It Is!

75

Beach Walk
By Karen S. Itin

Close your eyes. Create in your mind all the beauty this journey has to offer. This beach walk begins on a very long, wooden, weathered, white boardwalk running to the white sandy beach.

Once your feet hit the sand, you can feel the sand massaging your feet as you walk along the shoreline. The view of the navy-blue mass of water is breathtaking. The calm water and the sky meet on the horizon. There is nothing in between.

While continuing your walk, a large seashell appears. You stop to pick it up and take a seat in the sand. All unwanted thoughts overcome you as they flow out of you and into the seashell. You let go of any heartaches, and let the seashell hold them for now.

You leave the seashell there in the sand and begin to walk. You feel so calm. A scent of mint is in the air, and you can feel the mist of the water on your skin. You breathe in the freshness as it cleanses your body. The graceful sounds of the waves are hitting the shoreline. Smooth, teal beach glass starts to appear in front of you. Each small piece of glass is a letter in your name, and you walk until you have collected every letter.

This walk today was just what you needed. You feel grounded and refreshed like never before. You start to walk back toward the seashell you left behind. When you reach the seashell, you pick it up and take it with you. Now you have a place to deposit any unwanted thoughts at any time. You walk back across the boardwalk and slowly open your eyes, ready to begin your peaceful day.

76

Healthy Boundaries Meditation
By Kris Groth

I start my day by grounding to the earth through my feet, bringing earth energy up through the center core of my being, then continuing up through the top of my head to the heavens, and back into me. The loving energy of heaven and earth flows through me.

Divine light fills me, flowing into my core, and then through my entire body.

I allow light to radiate from within me, expanding out beyond my body, to the space around me, my energy field. I take time to feel it, sense it, and know it. This light assists me in reinforcing my energy field and patching any holes. I see it being repaired and strengthened.

Now, with my energy field secure, I set my energetic boundaries. These boundaries help establish my comfort level with others, and regulate what I allow into my energy field and what is kept out. This includes other people's energy, emotions, and anything that doesn't serve me. I have complete control over these boundaries. These settings can be checked and modified at any time, for any situation or circumstance.

Take a moment to set each boundary or intention, as specific as possible, visualizing and sensing each one ...

What does the boundary look and feel like? (Example: thickness, pliability, permeability, texture, distance from body)
Visualize, sense and know.

What do I want to block or keep out? (Example: negativity)

What do I want to sense and be aware of, but not bring in?
(Example: danger, other's emotions)

What do I want to accept and allow?
(Example: love, positivity)

I feel these healthy boundaries and intentions becoming firmly established and integrated into my mind, body and spirit. They are part of me. I move forward with my day knowing that I am safe, confident and strong!

And so it is.

77

Spirit Guided Day
By Lisa Hardwick

Place yourself in a way you are most comfortable.

Allow yourself to focus on your breath and become aware of the movement of your body as you inhale ... and as you exhale.

Now make a conscious effort to breathe more deeply. In through your nose, and hold it for a few seconds, and out through your mouth.

Keep breathing deeply, in through your nose, and hold for a few seconds, and pushing all thoughts that do not serve you ...
out through your mouth.

If you notice any uncomfortable thoughts ... simply release any judgment of yourself and direct your focus back to your breath.

This time, as you inhale ... say to yourself, "I Am" ... pause for a few seconds, and as you exhale ... say to yourself, "Relaxed."

Feel your body become more and more relaxed.

Now just breathe naturally as you picture a ray of white light from Spirit flowing down from the sky.

Notice Spirit's light as it streams down directly to your hand.

Feel the warmth of the light as it absorbs your entire palm.

Now take your light-filled palm ... and place it directly on your heart.

Visualize the light filling and warming your entire heart center.

Notice how much better you feel. Notice how your entire body is so much more relaxed.

You now have a 'knowing' that Spirit
is guiding your day ... in every way.

Every person you connect with – Spirit is there.

Every task is immersed with assistance from Spirit.

Every decision you make is Spirit infused.

If you find yourself needing strength somewhere within your day ...
simply place your hand on your heart and focus on your breath,
and Spirit will bring you the connection you seek.

78

A Love Like God's Love
By Karen Cowperthwaite

Take this time in silence, to drop into your heart. Notice this part of you, this inner compass, that knows what love feels like and seeks to find its presence.

In this moment, by choosing love to guide you, you will be given the clear direction you long for. Today, in all of its beauty and distraction, may you be centered in the awareness of a love like God's love.

Lord, help me to allow the challenges and embrace the part of me who feels so small and burdened.

Lord, help me to see fewer obstacles in my life and to give away more blessings.

Lord, help me to accept the support of others with a deep sense of gratitude, learning to accept my own helplessness and limitations.

Lord, help me to release the grip of panic when my heart is heavy. Within this sea of thoughts, allow me to be buoyed upward and reconnect with your wisdom.

Lord, help me to think beyond judgment and comparison. Encourage me to forgive and accept others to make space for even more love.

Lord, help me to become wiser with humility and grace. Deepen my understanding of this human experience that I may be more compassionate.

Lord, help me to show up as a shepherd and to be the shepherd of my own soul. Holding space for my own heart is like holding space for a hundred thousand hearts.

Lord, help me to take care of myself and to raise my own vibration. Clearing my energy fills me with your presence and healing.

Lord, allow your love to guide and transform me. With my every breath, help me to return to love, so that each and every day, I may experience a love like your love.

79

Let Your Choices Reflect Your Hopes, Not Your Fears

By Sandy Turkington

Today, I will be mindful of my thinking. I have lived my life fearful, preparing for the worst things to happen. As I do this, negative mind chatter and fear consume me. Why am I doing this to myself?

I can change the way I think at any time, so I choose to do so today. Please help me today, to look at all the good that surrounds me. Today, I will not let fear enter into my life. Today, I will be grateful for all my positive choices. I will see my hopes and dreams with openness and love. I will not fall back into fear. I will stay in the present moment.

Please teach me, angels, to remain strong ... to live and see my hopes and dreams with the best outcome and love possible. With each step, I can feel your strength and I embrace your love.

Today is a good day, and I welcome it with positivity and love.

80

Walking Towards Strength
By Kallie Johnston

Close your eyes.

Breathe.

Imagine you are driving. You turn off the main road, onto a dirt road atop a grassy hill. You start your descent down the hill. You feel the car's angle gradually increase. You slow your speed. As the pull gets stronger, you slow more. Slowly, slowly you reach the bottom.

Good job. Breathe.

Imagine you park the car in the middle of nowhere, just an empty, grassy area. You leave your car and take a walk through the grass. It's taller than you thought. You feel the top of it on your fingertips. It's soft, almost fuzzy. You continue walking. You see a lone flower.
A bright red flower. As you walk towards it, the breeze picks up.
It rushes past loudly in your ears. It sings along the grass.
You reach the flower, and the breeze dies.

You can now feel the warm sun on your cheek. You bend down and breathe in the strong scent of the flower. The sweet scent hits your nose and fills you up. You recognize that this is a safe space for you. You feel empowered in this state. Taking in a deep breath, you fill your lungs up with this clean air. You let out a hard breath, expelling your worries with it. You feel your strength now filling your lungs. It's effect is strong inside you. You let go of your anxiety, allowing you to be more creative.

You feel the need to dance. As you spin, your worries spin off of you. Taking another deep breath in, you feel ready to use your strength to face the day's challenges. You walk through the field once again, happier for the experience. You get in the car, feeling calm, centered, and ready to create an amazing day.

81

Peace Within Me
By Karen S. Itin

Peace comes from a place of being quiet and still within yourself. Sit and close your eyes and open your arms slightly. Imagine the type of peace your heart desires.

Only you know what type of peace you want. Say to yourself: "I am open to receive peace in my body, and peace in my heart."

I am open to receive peace in my breath, and in my movement. I welcome peace because it soothes me.

I am open to show peace in the words I speak to others, and in the actions I take towards them. I desire a peaceful life.

Picture yourself now as peaceful as you have ever felt yourself before. Envision yourself with that same peace right now. Apply that peace to your lifestyle. Breathe peacefully, and blow out slowly.

Reflect on what peace means to you. It may be to slow down your daily routine … Spend more time with the people who count ... Sometimes more time like this to yourself gives you all the peace you need. Breathe it in, and blow out slowly.

This renewed peace within yourself gives you the confidence you need. Breathe slowly and repeat these words:

At this moment, peace lives in me.

I am peace.

I am calm.

I am able to give, peacefully.

This peace I give to you.

And so it is.

82

Today I Am New
By April L. Dodd, M.A.

Today I am new.

This is my only job today,

To be new.

It is my inheritance,

And I claim it as the truth about me.

I am New.

For as newness, I am alive.

And for this, I am grateful.

As newness itself, I have endless possibilities.

Through these eyes, I see everything newly.

Through these hands, I am a conduit of light.

Through this heart, I am alive with the pulse of Spirit,

Surrounding me, encasing me, cocooning me

In the warmth of Heaven's promise.

Everything I would want is available to me,

And I would not place my value in futile substitutions of my truth.

To be new is to put my focus on my own breath, for it is mine alone.

Within it holds everything I would need in this now.

It does not hold the past, for it does not exist now.

It does not concern itself with the future, for only this moment is real.

It does not make choices on what to love, for everything is an opening to the heart I share with God.

It is a privilege to be new, not a guarantee.

It is something I must nurture if I want to grow.

Something I must allow to emerge through me,

In its fullest expression

If I would want to be fully alive.

Safe in the breath of Spirit,

I am a unique celebration of the will of God.

83

Bring Forth Your Light
By Dawn Michele Jackson

As you begin your morning, let go of any unpleasant thoughts. Perhaps there are thoughts left over from yesterday or even worries about the future. Bring yourself to the present moment, the only moment you have before you. Take a few deep breaths as you feel yourself relaxing into your being. Allow a sense of peace to sweep through you. Focus on your breathing while you feel your light within growing larger. See the light expanding out from your heart, traveling to each corner and crevice of your physical body. Know that with each breath your light is growing, as you are also dropping into an even greater space of serenity, balance and peace.

What is coming up for you? Are there still thoughts creeping in, trying to interrupt this beautiful moment? Slowly breathe them out. Know that today is all that you have right now. Yesterday is gone, tomorrow is to come. Today your light, in its entirety, will create a change in the world. It's your light that touches the Universe, and even you can feel it. It is this light that touches and supports others, while also drawing us together. There is connection in our light and that connection often tells us we aren't alone.

What would you like to do with your light today? How would you like to make a difference? There is no need to focus on something beyond your reach at this moment. Focus on the small ways your light can be extended outside of your physical form, and how it can touch those around you. Allow that part of you that never dies to become larger, and allow its brilliance to be felt. You are of great importance in this world. Your light is your magnificent beautiful soul, radiating. Shine brightly, my friend.

84

Awakening the Mystic Heart
By Ellen Elizabeth Jones

The golden white light of the Christ star within me now streams through my consciousness and cleanses every cell of this body in healing light.

The Christ light now dissolves and clears from me all fears, insecurities, angers and unresolved conflict.

Divine Love and Grace now pour through me and create an irresistible magnetic current of pure goodness.

I now see only perfection –
in myself, others, nature and the entire Cosmos.

I now draw to me all that is mine by divine right of consciousness.

Blessings are my truth, as I demonstrate through grace, hope and peace.

I am a master co-creating my treasure map that contains my joy, gifts and talents.

I call upon my ancestors and rightfully claim my divine inheritance.

I am powerful and wise.

I am free to be ALL of me!

I am in perfect alignment for all that is in my highest and greatest good.

With infinite love and appreciation, I stand upon sacred ground.

I embrace the I AM.

And So It Is!

85

Good Morning, Sunshine!

By Shalini Saxena Breault

Breathe into your abdomen –
Inhale love,
Exhale peace.

~ Two more breathing cycles here ~

Breathe in love,
Breathe out peace.

Keep your awareness on your abdomen and welcome in your inner light.

It's time for our light to wake up.

Breathe in love,
Breathe out kindness.

Breathe in love,
Breathe out radiance, feeling your light shine brighter.

Breathe in love,
Breathe out wholeness.

Breathe in love,
Breathe out illumination, feeling and connecting to your magnificence.

Breathe in love,
Breathe out fluidity.

Breathe in love,
Breathe out nourishment, feeling your light expand out.

Breathe in love,
Breathe out brilliance.

Breathe in love,
Breathe out rays of sunshine, feeling warmth in your heart.

Breathe in love,
Breathe out divinity.

Breathe in love,
Breathe out life, feeling your heart smile.

Breathe in love,
Breathe out worthiness.

Breathe in love,
Breathe out wisdom, REMEMBERING you are light ... SEEING the
light shine within and around you AS YOU!

Good Morning, Sunshine!

86

Seeking a Message from Above
By Adriana C. Tomasino

Envision yourself in the desert lands of the Sahara, where the sun is
burning brightly and there is nary a breeze. You feel an occasional
rippling in the sand as you proceed along your path. The grains of sand
remind you of the passage of time in an hourglass, as you visualize
Infinity lying on its side.

You can hear an unseen clock in your mind's eye—tick-tock-tick-tock,
and this reflects the very beat of your own heart. With every step you
take, you realize that water is scarce, and you still have an unknown
distance to travel. As you proceed, you have only the Divine with whom
to communicate. You ask, "Does life always need to be a struggle?" As
you begin to contemplate your own question, you see something in the
distance. You take for granted that this must be a mirage but continue
toward your imagined oasis anyway. As you approach, you become
aware that there is no body of water, as you had secretly hoped, but there
is a half-hidden object in its place. It is brown in hue, and appears to be a
bit darker than the sand. You bend down to pick it up, wondering, "What
could possibly survive here?"

As you wipe away the sand obscuring it, you recognize your seashell
from many years ago—a Tropidophora Land Snail—one that brings back
memories of days long past. Incredibly, something is tucked inside the
shell, and you remove a piece of parchment. There is writing, in the form
of hieroglyphics, scrawled upon it. As you struggle to read it, you realize
you are able to comprehend its message because it speaks directly to
your soul. It simply says: "You are on the right path. Life need not be
difficult so long as you follow your heart."

87

Dawn

By Susan Barrett

I honor the Dawn as a new beginning.

I leave behind all that has passed.

I leave ahead all that is future.

I feel the perfect serenity of being in the present.

I let go of what no longer serves me, without judgement.

I honor Mother Earth and all she provides.

I connect with the energy of the Earth and all other beings
to create harmony.

I will use my energy to transmute the negative energies around me.

I know tomorrow there will be another gift, of the Dawn.

88

My Heart Opens

By Lisa A. Clayton

My heart opens to the light of this new day with hope
and supernatural trust.
My heart opens to knowing there are unlimited possibilities
of opportunities.
My heart opens to courageous acts needed to move forward.
My heart opens to choosing love over fear.

My heart opens to bring a smile to each person I meet today.
My heart opens to singing a joyful song for no reason.
My heart opens to humming a soothing tune to calm me
when stress builds.
My heart opens to taking rest when my body guides me to slow down.

My heart opens to helping someone unexpectedly, without conditions.
My heart opens to each small compassionate act I can deliver.
My heart opens to feeling and showing empathy to others.
My heart opens to forgiveness when it feels sadness
or hears hurtful news.

My heart opens to calm and ease for harmony in all my responses.
My heart opens to receiving each interaction and conversation
with graceful listening.
My heart opens to radiating appreciation and care to all beings.
My heart opens to being an instrument of peace for this changing world.

My heart opens to the stars above shining universal harmony.
My heart opens to the Sun giving sustenance of life.
My heart opens to the Moon's mystery glowing in darkness.
My heart opens to Mother Earth magically delivering
beautiful gifts of nature.

My heart opens to greater self-love.
My heart opens to higher, Divine love.
My heart opens to unconditional love.
My heart opens to giving, receiving and being love.

My heart opens.

And so it is.

89

Morning Meditation for
a Peaceful Planet

By Allison Hayes, The Rock Girl®

Dearest Gaia, please speak to me ...

I hear you calling, I am ready now.

May we all gather and come together once again.

We have Re~awakened ...

To Remember ~ Recollect ~ Rebuild ~ and Revitalize our Souls.

May we Recall ~ Rediscover ~ Review ~ and Renew
our vows to Mother Earth.

May we Love thy Stones, Honor thy Trees, Respect thy Waters
~ and Connect our Souls.

Blessed be.

** This Morning Meditation was channeled in the heart of the Blue Ridge
Mountains, one of the oldest mountains in the world. The use of the word
"we" throughout this meditation is to promote a positive connection to
Souls across the Planet, and to Mother Gaia as well. This meditation can
be done individually, in groups, in person or remotely, as its ultimate
goal is to unite Souls throughout the Globe. When read aloud, and
accompanied by any stone of your choice, this meditation can be quite a
powerful experience!*

90

Be True to Yourself
By Julie Geigle

Take a deep breath, creating a beautiful, sacred space. Open up and engage the energy that is here for you, allowing this expansion to fill the deepest spaces of your soul.

Activating ~ Accelerating ~ Attuning

Letting go of all fears ... Releasing all expectations and attachments to the outcome. Feel the freedom you experience when you are in full and complete alignment with your Highest Self.

Place your hand on your heart and open up to give and receive the love that you are.

Oftentimes you may take action from a place of fear. You may give your power away wanting to please other people. Your own truth gets lost.

Imagine letting go of people, of things, of experiences that are holding you back and dragging you down.

As you open your heart to receive all that you are, it becomes easy and effortless to make decisions, to surround yourself with people who are supporting you.

The fog is being lifted on infinite levels and layers of your being.

If you need to ask yourself, "Should I or Shouldn't I?" within a relationship, job or experience, your lesson is not complete. For when it is time for you to leave you will INSTANTLY know and automatically take action.

Get true with yourself and watch as everything else in your life
magically falls into place.

You no longer need to ask others for advice, you no longer wonder
which way to turn. You are always instantly guided by your inner voice.

Stand in your power. See the truth of who you are … a glorious,
magnificent being with endless possibilities that await you NOW.

Feel your energy rising, continuing to expand and open to receive all that
you are and all that you came here to become.

Your truth is your North.

Channeled meditation by Metatron.

91

Meditation for Connecting to Nature and the Animals

By Jan Schipman

Begin your day in nature, walking barefoot on the grass.

Sit under a tree and call in the Angels, the nature spirits,
and all of the animals. Ask your animal companion to sit with you.
Connecting heart-to-heart, you are all joined together in a circle of
healing energy. BE in the moment. BE in the Now. You are all ONE.

Take a deep breath to get centered in your heart space. Breathe slowly, in
through your nose and out through your mouth (with sound, to help
move the energy). Take another deep smooth breath, knowing this will
return you to your center. Here you will be able to hear the messages
coming to you.

Sit quietly, listening to what the animals and nature are telling you. Look
around and notice the trees, grass, rocks, insects, birds, sky and clouds.
Take in all that nature and the animals are showing you.

Take another deep breath. Ask the angels to surround you with their
white light. Thank the Angels.
Ask the animals to surround you with their beautiful, loving and
compassionate energy. Thank the animals.
Feel the healing energy of nature surrounding you with glowing green
healing light. Be thankful to all of nature.
Know that you can come back to this circle anytime during the day. Be
in gratitude for this sacred space you are in. Feel the Love.

Take another deep cleansing breath and release. Be grateful for this
beautiful day, nature, the angels and the animals.

And So It Is…

92

Remembering My Gaian
Green Warrior Self
By Zing Nafzinger

Ah, my being is so vast materially that the cosmos is hard put
to contain it...

Ah, the star that I emerged from is so vast it is beyond my conception...

How can I ponder my bigness when I'm facing the challenges of every
day—what to eat, what to wear, how to smile and say hello to these
people around me?

I don't want to pretend I am small.

My Gaian Green Warrior Self is so strong that I need never fear it not
being there for me. I can lean on my Self for support. I feel its strength.

As I imagine one of the challenges I will face today—a mountain to
move, a hole to fill—I ask myself what is more important, that I feel the
strength of my Self, or that the hole get filled?

I am aligned with my Self when I feel that it is more useful to feel the
Presence of my Self than for me to accomplish a specific task!

In this moment, I give up my burdens. I focus on the state of my heart
center. Do I feel peace? Do I feel at peace with my neighbors?

What would it take for me to become a Gaian Green Warrior in every
aspect of my life—my cooking, my sleeping, my love-making? What
would it mean for me to so steadfastly seek Presence over
Accomplishment that I would willingly transform my way of being in the
world—seeking to experience Presence in every moment of my day.

I feel my strength. I open my heart. I accept the challenge of living a life of Presence—presence to my planet Earth, presence to my neighbors, loved ones, and friends, and presence to all the aspects of my life.

93

Lavender Aroma
By Karen S. Itin

Let your mind drift to a large, beautiful lavender garden. A sea of purple lavender plants lined up in perfect rows for as far as your eyes can see. The colorful plants are perfect in form and beautiful in nature. Breathe it all in, and let it out softly.

You begin to walk along the rows, crushing with your feet the buds that have fallen to the ground. The aroma you smell is so sweet, that with each breath you take, you become more and more relaxed. Your neck now feels relaxed, and your shoulders start to feel loose. Tensions begin to flow out of you. Just breathe softly.

You notice that your arms and legs are very relaxed as you bend over to pick a lavender flower bud. You begin to break apart the bud, and it amazes you that such a tiny piece of the flower is so potent with lavender aroma. The smell of the lavender is all you can detect as it takes over your whole body, and soothes you.

Your mind feels refreshed and free, as you decide to start harvesting some of the lavender to take home. You begin walking with a basket you find sitting on the ground. You pull off some of the flower buds and place them in the basket. You realize what a beautiful walk this is, as you return slowly back to the porch and place the basket next to the door.

While sitting next to the basket, you take in the lavender aroma. Your mind now feels fresh and sharp, and you are ready to start your day. The lavender gives you a feeling of being deeply connected with nature. You look forward to visiting this garden again and again.

94

Today … I Breathe … Let Go … and Have Gratitude …

By Deb Frischmon

Sit in a comfortable position … sitting up tall … lifting the top of your head up towards the sky … lengthening your spine.

Take a deep slow breath in … filling up all four corners of your belly … gently hold it … release with an audible sigh … relaxing … letting go.

Take another deep breath in … hold it … release … letting go … opening your heart center.

Take one more deep breath in … hold it … letting go … being open to new possibilities.

Setting intentions for your day … silently stating …

"Today is a good day."

"Today I let go of any worry … releasing my worries to the angels … trusting all is well."

"Today I let go of doubt … believing in me … not giving up … believing anything is possible."

"Today I let go of judgment … letting go of judging myself … or finding fault with others."

"Today I let go of fear … having more courage … embracing change."

"Today I let go of having to please everyone … being true to myself."

"Today I trust that what I feel in my heart is right … listening to my intuition … the still small voice inside."

"Today I have positive thoughts … remembering when I'm positive … I attract more positive."

"Today I take care of me … making me a priority … slowing down … going within … connecting with spirit … doing what I love … saying no… eating mindfully … moving my body … getting enough rest."

"Today is a new day … a day I surrender … trusting that I'm always guided and loved … more than I can even imagine."

"Today … I let go … and I let God … allowing magic … miracles … and synchronicities … into my life."

"Today I feel my vibration … going higher … feeling love … joy … peace … freedom …"

"Today I appreciate life … feeling deep … deep … gratitude."

"Thank you … thank you … thank you … I am so blessed!"

Love and light!

Namasté

95

A New Day to Choose a New Vibration
By Paula Obeid

A new day to create a new vibration. A new day to appreciate life more fully. A new day to know that I AM HUMAN, and ALL IS WELL. A new day to reach for the highest vibrational thought I CAN CHOOSE. A new day that I KNOW all is happening for my highest good. A new day to take time to AFFIRM and APPRECIATE that I AM LOVE and

I AM ALL these things:

I AM SELF-LOVING.

I AM RELENTLESS.

I AM PERFECTION.

I AM PASSIONATE.

I AM INTUITIVE.

I AM SUPPORTED.

I AM POWERFUL.

I AM ABUNDANT.

I AM GRATEFUL.

I AM WELLNESS.

I AM RESILIENT.

I AM COMPLETE.

I AM PURE LOVE.

A new day to create a new vibration. A new day to appreciate life more fully. A new day to know that I AM HUMAN and ALL IS WELL. A new day to reach for the highest vibrational thought I CAN CHOOSE. A new day to know that all my life experiences help define the magnificent soul that I AM. A new day to know who I AM & shout it from the mountain tops: I am! I Am!! I AM!!!

96

Morning Meditation: Bubble of Love
By Terri Beaver

Sit back or lie down, relax and make yourself comfortable.

Breathe in love, and out fear; thinking, "I am safe."

Repeat five times.

Tense all of your muscles from your ears to your toes. Relax and let go.

Repeat five times.

Say in your mind: "I am strong, I am worthy, I matter."

Repeat five times.

Imagine that you are in a bubble of protection, nothing can harm you.

This bubble can take you any place you want to go,
controlled by your mind.

You instantly go to a distant planet that is filled with love and light.

Happiness visibly shines in the air, with an effervescent beam of white
glittery joy and unconditional love.

You feel safe and leave the bubble; you are greeted with many smiles.

"We are happy to finally see you here," they say.

"We have been waiting for you for such a long time."

Each being greets you with a warm familiar hug.

You are taught how to overcome pain and illness with love.

You trustingly breathe in love, out pain.

You are healthy and pain free.

You are ready.

You now meet your spiritual guide who will mentor you in life on earth.

Your mentor only guides you when asked, keeping you safe with soft whispers, allowing you to follow your path, without judgement.

You get in your bubble with him/her; seeing the magical possibilities for you, as you head towards home, to live life more fully, fearlessly.

You have arrived to the place where it is safe to be you, protected with unconditional love.

You love yourself, accept yourself and trust yourself with your life.

You are looking forward to all of life's challenges and transitions; knowing you are always loved and safe. You are never alone.

97

Practice Mindfulness
By Katina Gillespie Ferrell

Improving quality of mind begins with clearing negativity. It is not something that you 'do' or squeeze into your life. There is not a one size 'checklist' that fits everyone. It's about letting go of the items and thoughts that block realizing your true nature and creating your best life! Your mind is a powerful thing. When you fill it with positive thoughts, your life will begin to change. Let's cultivate compassion and love for all.

Think of your brain as a muscle, and thoughts are like lifting weights. A few changes in thought will change the outcome. Consider focusing on one mental factor at a time. Still your mind and focus on that one virtuous object for five minutes every morning and carry that intent throughout the day. Perfect practice makes perfect. Avoid a result driven practice. It is practice, not a destination. In our morning mindfulness practice, we are creating cause and encouraging our minds toward inner peace and happiness. Distractions will arise, and you will lose focus. Gently return to the object of the meditation.

Stop and remember: Whatever is going on in your mind is what you are attracting. It's the Law of Attraction. Mindset is everything! Keep your mind positive and good things will come. Be mindful of being a victim of negative self-talk and remember … YOU are listening! Forget all the reasons why it won't work and concentrate on why it WILL work! Remind yourself of the physical and mental benefits of meditation.

Thinking about our mental delusions is our greatest addiction. Break the habit! Think about your joys!!! After your morning meditation, record something positive each day in your journal and carry that positive throughout your day!

Namasté!

98

Loving Pink Mist of Light
By Trish Bowie

Close your eyes and get yourself into a comfortable position.

Now ... take a few deep breaths, in through your nose,
and out your mouth.

If there is tension in your body or heaviness in your heart,
just give a big sigh,

Letting go of all your worries and concerns.

Take a minute to ask your heart what it needs; see if there is anything
you can do for it.

If there are any feelings that come up, just allow them to be there ... you
don't need to do anything with them.

Now ... visualize a pink mist of light showering your body with love.

Feel the pink light as it travels through the top of your head, down your
throat, and into your heart center.

Continue on down to your feet.

Now ... allow that pink mist of light to travel back up your body
to your heart.

Send it down your arms and out your hands.

As it comes out of your hands, visualize that you are directing it to your
loved ones or to a place in need of healing.

Then, bring your hands back to your heart and fill yourself with this healing and loving pink mist of light.

Continue this for as long as it is comfortable to give and receive love.

When you are ready ... slowly open your eyes, and become aware of your environment.

Bow, and give blessings for this beautiful day.

99

Loving Kindness
By Halina Kurowska

Assume a comfortable position ... Allow your body to be relaxed and your mind quiet ... Direct your attention to your breath ... inhale ... fill yourself with life-giving air ... exhale .... and relax ....

Now ... consciously focus your attention on your heart area .... The feeling of loving kindness is the feeling you have for a newborn baby, a puppy, a kitten ... anything that arises the soft loving feeling in your heart ... start with this feeling ... hold onto it ... then offer this love to yourself ... your loved ones ... extending it to all sentient beings ... and to the whole world ....

Feel your breath totally merging with your heart ...

Begin with yourself ...

May I be filled with loving kindness ... be happy ... healthy ... peaceful ... safe ... and ... live with love ... ease and wellbeing ...

Now ...direct your attention to your loved ones ...

May you be filled with loving kindness ... be happy ... healthy ... peaceful ... safe ... and ... live with love ... ease and wellbeing ...

Now ... expand this feeling of love and compassion coming out from your heart even further ... to your friends ... neighbors ... include the difficult people in your life ... this might not be easy at the beginning ... but try ... take a first step towards compassionate love ... feel this LOVE and COMPASSION emanating from your beautiful radiant heart and spreading to the whole world ...

Say, "May all beings be filled with loving kindness ... be happy ... healthy ... peaceful ... safe ... and free."

Sit with this wonderful feeling of LOVE filling your whole Being and expanding and embracing the whole world ...

Namasté

100

We Are One - Morning Salutation to Mother Earth

By Shanda Trofe

Upon rising, stand to the east, feet firmly planted on the ground, legs shoulder width apart, arms open, palms facing up.

Close your eyes and take a deep breath in … hold it … and release …

Imagine now, energetic roots growing out of the bottoms of your feet, down deep into Mother Earth until they reach and wrap around the energy of Her core.

Visualize the center of the earth emanating a radiant colorful glow, and trust that whatever color you are called to draw up into you is exactly what you need in this moment.

Deep breath in, draw this colorful energy of Mother Earth up into you, until it reaches your heart-center.

Now, visualize your Crown Chakra opening wide, while the heavenly light of the Divine streams down and fills you with a golden-white light until it meets the earth energy in your Heart Chakra.

Swirling and blending together, these two energies mix and spin until your Heart Chakra opens wide and light radiates out of you.

Light spills from your heart-center, covering the entire earth and all of Her inhabitants, connecting you to all things in this moment.

Visualize this light healing our planet, all the while allowing these powerful energies to continue to stream through you …

Feel the joy and love in your heart now, knowing we are all One.

Open your eyes, empowered and ready to start the day.

Place your hand upon your heart and repeat…

And so it is!

101

The Bicycle of Inner Peace
By Charles Ferrell

Many things in life can be taught, and some only experienced. The mechanics of riding a bike can be broken down into teachable steps, but balance only comes with experience. In the same way, meditation posture and breath awareness are taught, while inner peace comes from the experience created through practice. There is good reason it is called a meditation practice, not a meditation perfection. The distractions of the mind come and go at all stages of experience.
There are no bad meditation sessions and no failures.

Meditation always has an object; it is an act of focus, not a lack thereof. The object of focus is our point of gentle return from distractions, our center. As our handle bars of focus may swing wildly from side to side at first, the more we peddle (practice) the easier it is to steer to center. Focusing on an outward object like the breath is where we begin; but at times, the wild mind wanders far and wide. Just like a child on its first bike, there are meditative training wheels that can help us to keep peddling through a distracted mind. We can take the object of practice more into the physical realm by using Mantra. The word Mantra literally means "Mind Protection", the simple nature of mantra distracts us from our distractions.

Any simple positive phrase or ancient Sanskrit can be used:
"Om Ah Hum" or "I am love" or "I am peace"

Take any string of beads, the first bead between the thumb and forefinger. Speak the mantra aloud or in your mind once.
Move to the next bead and repeat.

Most of all, Keep Peddling.

102

A Growing Seed

By Neen Forder

Our souls and our lives go through cycles, just as a flower grows each year. I'd like you to imagine that you are a plant in the border of a beautiful garden. Your mission is simply to BE; and if you wish, to grow here in whatever way feels right for you.

Feel your roots sinking into the moist soil beneath your feet. Feel the warming light of the sunshine in the crystal blue sky above you. You're aware that there are other plants around you, some bigger, some smaller. You feel completely nurtured and safe as you lift your chin slightly to reach up towards the warm and nourishing sunshine, and know you have room to grow.

Each plant, including you, has been lovingly placed so you have space to grow into your full potential, when you're ready. Notice where you are in your cycle of growth now, and breathe into that energy. Are you a small seedling about to spring into life, a young plant about to have a growth spurt? Are you a flower bud about to unfold your beauty, showing both your strength and your delicate structure? Or are you a mature flower with a ripe seed-head about to gently burst and spread your wisdom and knowledge far and wide? Or perhaps you are ready to pull in your energy and hibernate until next year? Know that you are safe and you are exactly at the right stage of your development for you right now.

You help make this garden beautiful. You have everything you need to continue your growth when you're ready, and you're fully in charge of the nutrients you take in. But for now, all you have to do, is focus on where you are right now and BE.

103

Fulfilling Water Meditation

By Cynthia Stoneman

Good morning, clear refreshing water. Thank you for awakening my senses with a clean fresh scent and warm caress from my head to my toes. Wash away all lingering energies from the night, along with any fears or insecurities. Refresh my mind, body and spirt to be ready for this new day. Fill my energy with joy, creativity and excitement.

Warm water glides across my skin and reminds me that every part of me is beautiful. All the little parts and all the big parts are a valued portion of my physical body. Rippling water reminds me that even in the smallest drop, the water has strength, and so do I. Going with the flow, water does not cling, it simply glides along its path. As droplets reach a crease or wrinkle, they gently and elegantly follow a path of grace and ease down to my toes.

As the water ripples from my head to my toes, I affirm that I am strong and gentle, like the water. I nourish my body. I fill myself up with love, joy and understanding. I spend time in the present moment. Taking care of myself allows me to be of service today and in the next days.

As the water flows over me, it fills me with energy and support, to easily and joyfully move through the day.

104

Butterfly Messages

By Karen S. Itin

Sit at peace with yourself in a relaxed way. Close your eyes and imagine beautiful butterflies dancing around in your head. Renew your vision of how peaceful and fragile butterflies are. They come in many sizes, colors, and beautiful patterns. What if each time you saw a butterfly they had a message of goodness just for you? Just breathe.

A message of peace, and how to be peaceful toward others. A message of hope, and how to offer hope to the people around you. A message of comfort, and whoever you need to share it with. A message from above, that you are loved! Just breathe.

Butterflies have a very peaceful way of guiding us to reality. Many times, you see them land on flowers ... Telling us to take time to smell the flowers ... Take a moment to just breathe.

Let's imagine how many times butterflies have followed us around in our yards or gardens ... How they land right by us as if they have a message to share. What messages would they bring to you? Something like "You are beautiful?" Tell the butterflies what you would like to say to the universe. Give the butterflies a message now.
Something like: "Butterflies flying North and South, send the people there love and courage. Butterflies flying East and West, send the people there hope and peace."
Whatever loving message you want to send out
into the world, this will all come back to you too.
Now, just take a moment to breathe.

Reflect on the messages you just passed along to the butterflies.
Receive love and courage in your own heart.
Hope and peace will now guide you into your day.
And so it is.

105

Love and Accept Who You Are Morning Meditation - What A Way To Start Your Day

By Danielle Baker Dailey

I would like for you to start by finding a comfortable spot that feels good.

Once you are comfortable, go ahead and gently close your eyes, taking in a deep beautiful breath filled with love. Let that breath out slowly. Another deep beautiful breath in, really allowing your lungs to expand, filling them with love and gratitude, and then release. One last deep cleansing breath, feeling very grounded and safe, and let that breath out.

While keeping your eyes closed, go ahead and place your dominate hand over your heart and feel your heartbeat and connect with it. Once you feel it, smile and say out loud, "Thank you, thank you for all that you do for us." Visualize your heart opening up and smiling back at you. With your heart open, visualize light pouring out from your heart. Once you feel the expansion and the love coming in and out of your heart space, repeat: I AM choosing to love myself today. I AM open to loving and accepting myself exactly as I am. I AM willing to love who I am. I have decided to love and accept myself today and be my own very best friend. It is safe for me to love myself today. I AM giving myself permission to love myself.

If you feel any resistance around this, it's ok. Repeat until you feel more comfortable with this idea. Take three more deep beautiful breaths and say thank you, thank you, thank you.

Gently open your eyes and notice a lighter feeling throughout your day. You deserve to live with a peaceful mind!!

It is your birthright to live your best life, so go ahead and really embrace today.

106

Goddess Meditation

By Elayne Le Monde

I receive the great Goddess of Love and awaken to the grandeur that I am. This day I walk in absolute trust of the All-Knowing that dwells within.

I am a sacred witness of all creation and the reflection of reverence reveals its holiness through me. I trust the ever-unfolding grandeur of grace. Like a kaleidoscope, I evolve and expand into each new experience witnessing the colors and hues of my Being.

Pure Source reveals to me Divine Will and my words are a sacred mantra to the place where truth and integrity reside.

The quiet whisperings of my heart guide me freely to the next right step that radiates my brilliance in surrender to the unknown.

I embody the passion that drives me to live through my heart flame and know the ecstasy of the celestial dance. Life simply beckons me to embrace the moment as I honor each breath as Love.

I am the Master of my frequency, there is nothing bigger than I Am. I honor the wisdom of my Soul and acknowledge co-creation with Source.

I live in Divinity and purpose, accepting the perfection of my Soul's plan. Alchemy is the transcendence of my perceptions to the brightest outcome and the ever-expanding holiness that is my birthright.

I lovingly release my mind, as stillness is my sanctuary and solace. I forgive the judgment of my perceptions and watch in fascination to the unveiling synchronicity and alignment of my deepest desires.

I am an awakened warrior of truth and honor. My Light shines brightly as I carry the torch of illumination for the path of unification with the Beloved. As ONE, I anchor the radiance of Love in the crystalline heart of Gaia and pulsate her highest octave of purity through my veins.

107

Live in Harmony with the Elements
By Karen J. Lewis

When you return to a physically awakened state in the morning, rather than bringing to mind the tasks for the day ahead, try using this short, yet powerful, ritual to honor yourself, your day, and our life-sustaining elements.

Ideally, perform this ritual immediately as you get out of bed and your feet touch the floor, while you are still experiencing the soft and drifty lull of your peaceful awakening to the day.

Face the north, feeling the earth supporting you.
Take one step forward and say, "I honor and embrace the divine earth and feminine energy of the north."
Bow in gratitude.

Step back to center and take a deep accepting breath. Allow yourself to receive the energetic gifts of Mother Earth in this moment.

Next, turn to the east. Take one step forward and say, "I honor and embrace the breath of life and renewal from the sacred east."
Bow in gratitude.

Step back to center and take a deep accepting breath. Feel the energy from the air you breathe and allow it to nourish your body.

Turn now to the south. Take one step forward and say, "I honor and embrace the sacred element of fire and passion from the south."
Bow in gratitude.

Step back to center and take a deep accepting breath, as you feel the warm energy of fire.

Turn now to the west. Take one step forward and say, "I honor and embrace the emotions and reflections of water from the west."

Bow in gratitude.

Step back to center and take a deep accepting breath, as you allow the energy of water to heal, soothe and flow through you.

Today, I will live in harmony with the elements and embrace the gifts and sustenance they lovingly provide.

And so it is!

108

The Gifts of the Doors

By Nancy Newman

Give yourself three deep, slow breaths to relax. Close your eyes and in your mind's eye imagine you are in a hallway representing your life path, which meanders and stretches in both directions as far as you can see.

As you begin walking, notice there are countless doors in varied sizes with assorted colors and different handles. Some are open, some shut. Some welcoming, some intimidating.

The ones nearest to you are past experiences which are ready to be left behind. Some may already be resolved, but there are still several you may consider examining today. As you choose one, what are the thoughts and limiting beliefs you are ready and willing to release which reside in this room? Are you willing to let go of your attachment to these things?

As you seal this door, give gratitude for the gifts and lessons this room gave to you, and acknowledge you are now willing to move beyond that story. Imagine yourself blessing and discharging those experiences before you move on.

You also see numerous other doors ready to reveal wonderful unfamiliar ways of believing and being! Walk forward along the path and examine the undiscovered knowledge just waiting for you. Look at the colors. Do any seem to have patterns or feel familiar? Are they warm and inviting, or do they seem scary? What different "patterns" and beliefs do you want to welcome into your life?

Confidently welcome a fresh way of thinking, knowing you are safe and protected. What does this feel like? Be sure to give thanks to the Universe for your new blessing! When you have received your gifts of the doors, open your eyes knowing this unique belief is now a part of you and your life – AND SO IT IS.

109

Balanced and Whole

By Lisa Hardwick

Place yourself in a comfortable position and breathe in through your nose for 4 seconds, pause for 7 seconds, and exhale slowly for 8 seconds.

Continue breathing the 4 – 7 – 8 sequence while placing your focus on your Heart Center.

Visualize a bright blue flame filling your Heart Center to clear anything that does not serve you.

Now, visualize the bright blue flame traveling from your Heart Center to your Mind, and clearing any negative thoughts you have about yourself or other people and replacing them with thoughts of love, compassion and gratitude.

You are now balanced and whole.

Now, say to yourself:

My Heart Center and Mind is filled with loving thoughts.

I look for beauty throughout my day.

I am guided and protected.

It is safe to speak my truth.

I live a life of gratitude.

I am productive.

I am radiant.

I am balanced and whole.

If during my day I notice a negative thought, I picture the thought as a balloon and I release it to disappear in the sky.

Continue to breathe in through your nose for 4 seconds, pause for 7 seconds, and exhale slowly for 8 seconds.

And again.

Breathe in through your nose for 4 seconds, pause for 7 seconds, and exhale slowly for 8 seconds.

As you bring your focus back to the room, be aware that you now have a "knowing" you are balanced and whole and you're well prepared to start your day.

110

I Am Enough

By Julie Geigle

I am perfect and whole. I do not need anyone
or anything to complete me. I am enough.

Take a deep breath and relax into this truth.

As I put myself first in my life, I create a beautiful relationship with my
Soul, the essence of who I am.

I let go of any attachments to wanting things to be different than they are.
I meet myself where I am at, with no condemnation,
criticism or judgment.

I am present in my life now.

I find the gifts that this present moment brings me.

I am whole and complete. I am an aspect of Divinity. There is nothing
broken and nothing needs to be fixed.

There is no one I need to complete me. I am completed.

I am the perfect and the perfection. I am the expression of God.

There is nothing that God needs to complete Himself, for He is the fullest
expression of all, of everything. There may be things that enhance that
expression but there is nothing that He desires,
for He is the all of everything, as AM I!

Sometimes I may get attached to my story of "I am not enough."

I call Angels 911, help me now to release my stories
and see with perfect clarity the truth of my being.

Releasing all attachments to my story, of feeling alone and incomplete.

I am a priority in my life.

I rise up and feel the love that God has for me in this moment,
the completeness of that which I am.

I take the time to love myself completely as God loves me…
unconditional, pure LOVE.

As I sink deeply into the truth of my essence, there arises a beautiful
serenity, a harmony with who I am ... strong, independent, self-sufficient.

I AM ENOUGH.

Channeled meditation from Metatron

111

Invocation of the Archangels:
A Guided Meditation
By Sunny Dawn Johnston

Begin by invoking Michael, the Archangel of protection. He stands to your right. You invite him in by saying "I now invoke the mighty and powerful blue light of Archangel Michael to surround me and protect me."

Next invoke the ruby red energy of Uriel to stand to your left side. "I now invoke the mighty and powerful Archangel Uriel. Please surround me with your wisdom, peace, and joy."

When you're feeling ready to invoke Archangel Raphael, begin by imagining a beautiful emerald-green energy completely enveloping you. "I now invoke the mighty and powerful Archangel Raphael to stand before me. Please surround me and fill me with health, well-being, and wholeness."

Feel Gabriel's pure white energy of communication and clarity. "I now invoke the mighty and powerful Archangel Gabriel to stand behind me. Please bring me insights and awareness so that I may always speak my truth."

Focus now on your heart center and the gentleness of Archangel Chamuel. "I now invoke the mighty and powerful pink light of Archangel Chamuel to expand the love I have in my heart. Please help me to find unconditional love and compassion for myself and others."

Now you see a beautiful golden-yellow energy encircling you, and you know that Archangel Jophiel is surrounding you. "I now invoke the powerful Archangel Jophiel to surround me in the golden light of beauty and manifestation.
Please help me see the world through eyes of beauty."

Finally, you find yourself supported by the violet ray of forgiveness and mercy, and you know that Archangel Zadkiel is present. "I now invoke the mighty Archangel Zadkiel to help me surrender and release any judgment, criticism, or neglect from myself or others. Please help me to find the value in all of life's experiences."

Now that you have invoked the Archangels, allow yourself to bathe
in their unconditional love, divine perfection, and peace
until you feel ready to begin your day.
You will experience miracles when you do this consistently.

Author Biographies

Adriana C. Tomasino is an Angel Communication Master, a Professional Seashell Reader, a doctoral candidate in medieval literature pursuing research on Hildegard von Bingen, a student of Dr. Jean Houston and President of Heaven Seas: Wings and Harps, a business dedicated to personal empowerment. Please e-mail her at dreemstar1@aol.com.

Allison Hayes, The Rock Girl® is an international, award-winning Psychic and founder of The Rock Girl Sacred Stone School. She travels worldwide as a Transformational Speaker, Empowerment Expert and Master Teacher, specializing in Personal Growth & Spiritual Transformation. Allison educates, motivates, inspires and empowers people across the globe! www.TheRockGirl.com; www.SacredStoneSchool.com.

Angela N. Holton is a Transformational Coach, Speaker, and Author. She is the founder of Love Sanctuary, an online spiritual and personal development site, centered on helping individuals create success and transformation. To learn more about Angela, visit her at www.lovesanctuary.com.

Ann Albers is a popular author, spiritual instructor, angel communicator, and modern mystic. Her free weekly "Messages from Ann & the Angels" reach an international audience with inspiration and tips to help you stay tuned in and turned on! Learn about her books, CDs, and Internet Television Show at www.visionsofheaven.com.

April-Anjali McCray is a Soul Healer and Woman of Empowerment! Through her soul healing sessions, healing classes and weekly radio show April-Anjali stands as a goddess of transformation, leading other women to awaken their inner healing power to grow heal and evolve beyond their wildest dreams. Her contact is www.April-Anjali.com.

April L. Dodd, M.A. is a best-selling author, award-winning actress, Life & Executive Coach of 17 years, and humbled mother. With an unshakeable passion for what's possible, April serves as a trusted confidant, eye-opening guide, and a breath of fresh air in creating massive change for an extraordinary life. www.aprildodd.com.

Bobbe Bramson is a gifted Angel Medicine Woman, healer, intuitive, author, spiritual teacher and ordained Angel Minister through Gateway University. Her unique healing strategies and transformational tools are designed to help people reconnect to their Divine Radiance and shine it into the world. Contact Bobbe: bramsongs@verizon.net or via www.AngelHeartToHeart.com.

Bonnie Larson is a Healing Minister, Reiki Healer, Lay Minister, published author and accomplished business executive. Her passion is to share insights, bridging the gap between religion and spirituality, enabling you to realize your highest possible potential. www.bonnielarson.net.

Carolan Dickinson is a psychic medium, angel communicator, teacher, and author of the book, *Walking with the Archangels* (Amazon, 2016). Her essay, *"The Magic of Healing with the Archangels,"* is featured in the anthology, Spiritual Leaders Top Picks (Visionary Insight Press 2017). www.carolandickinson.com.

Catherine Madeira: Bequeathed with information in Sciences, Space, Metaphysics, Clairvoyance and beyond. Knowledge shared through writing or request. Previous works found on Amazon & B&N. catherinemadeira@aol.com. Daughter of Lilas Hardin. Mother of Brilliant, Jason & Kendal Vaughan. Grand Mother of Cherished Harlo Monroe our Crystal Child.

Charles Ferrell has been practicing Buddhist meditation and Dharma for 15 years. He works in technology management. In his spare time, he teaches meditation and practices with his wife Katina in the New Kadampa Tradition.

Charmaine Gagnon is a Photographer, Writer, Poet, and Reiki Master. She loves nature and all of creation, and she expresses this with an open heart. As an empath, she feels what others feel, recognizes their true essence, and honors the Divinity in all people.

Cheryl Carrigan is a full-fledged peacock who loves to live her life in vivid 3D color and is inspired/guided by the Angels. She is an Inspirational Author, Speaker and Mentor, a Spiritual Teacher, and Psychic/Medium. www.cherylcarrigan.com.

Courtney Long, MSW, LC, CHt, ATP® is an Angel Communicator, Life Purpose Intuitive, Author, Speaker, Hypnotherapist, and Master's Level Social Worker. She inspires spiritual individuals to shine brightly, share their gifts, and fulfill their Divine Life Purpose in a passionate, prosperous way, with the help of the Angels and Fairies. www.CourtneyLongAngels.com.

Cris T Linn, author, student, and teacher of esoteric studies shares her knowledge through workshops and one on one coaching sessions. Believing the tools that saved her, can also save the world, she is expanding her message and dedicating her life to building a bridge of awareness to metaphysical modalities.

Cynthia Stoneman is blessed with a gift for having the words people need to hear, when they need to hear them. She is a Certified Mind, Body, Spirit Practitioner, Mastery Energy Healer, Intuitive Guide and Author. You can contact her via email at Cynthia.stoneman@gmail.com.

Danielle Baker Dailey is a licensed Heal Your Life teacher based on the philosophies of Louise Hay and a certified QSCA Law of Attraction coach. Through her own personal journey and experiences, it is her greatest passion to teach others how to empower themselves and live their greatest life. www.daileylifecoaching.com.

Dawn Michele Jackson is a registered nurse, grief recovery specialist, writer and practitioner of multiple healing modalities. As a Beautycounter consultant she's passionate about educating others regarding the safety of products used in their daily lives. Residing in Portland, Oregon she enjoys exploring the Pacific Northwest with those she loves. www.dawnmichelejackson.com.

Deb Alexander lives in Minnesota and works at a community center teaching Deep and Shallow Water Aerobics, swim lessons and yoga. Besides her family and friends, she enjoys her hens, Rufus the cat, creating art, and learning through life's journey.

Deb Frischmon is a spiritual teacher, speaker, mentor, and writer. Deb is also a yoga instructor, reiki practitioner, and numerology reader. She loves inspiring others, helping them learn, grow, heal, evolve, understand their life purpose, cultivate self-love, and live life fully being all they can be. www.debfrischmon.com.

Dr. Karen Maxwell - CEO of Euphoria Transformations and Maxwell Family Chiropractic Center. An innovative and progressive Chiropractor, Elite Master B.E.S.T. practitioner, Intuitive Healer, Medium and Transformational licensed Heal Your Life® workshop leader and coach. Specializing in complete wellness, where her retreats and wellness programs are focused on changing lives. www.drkarenmaxwell.com.

Elayne Le Monde is the founder of Empower Wholeness Transformational Retreats, Quantum Holographic Intuitive, an Advanced Practitioner of Neuro Energetic Kinesiology, Transformational Coach; specializing in distance sessions. Mother of five children, Elayne resides in Kailua-Kona, Hawaii. She enjoys swimming and island adventures offering Mastery retreats. www.EmpowerWholeness.com.

Ellen Elizabeth Jones is a spiritual teacher, mystic messenger, speaker and author. Ellen's passion is to empower others through private sessions, workshops, and retreats to embrace and trust the wisdom of their own heart, inspiring them to live a life of Peace, Love and Joy! www.ellenelizabethjones.com; ellen@ellenelizabethjones.com.

Georgia Nagel is an Animal Communicator and number one best-selling author. She just released her first book *Pet Talker (Listening to those who speak silently)*. Georgia loves to educate people on their pets and what they can do to make their lives better by interacting with them and Nature. www.georgianagel.com.

Gina Barbara offers a unique coaching and energetic healing style to motivated clients wishing to flourish in authentic lives; and to nurture and nourish themselves, others and the planet. Counseling Cert; Dip Transpersonal Life Coaching; Colour Therapy LV 111; Crystal Healing Cert, EFT Cert. and many other healing modalities. www.innerselfcare.com.

Giuliana Melo is a spiritual teacher, angel intuitive, Goddess energy practitioner, and author. She is married for 30 years and has a 19-year-old son. She lives and loves in Calgary AB Canada. She loves being of service. www.giulianamelo.com.

Halina Kurowska is an author, Life Coach, Spiritual Counsellor, Heal Your Life® Teacher and founder of Living With AWE: Awareness Wisdom Empowerment. Halina has spent many years on a path of spiritual development. Having transcended her life, she is now assisting others in their transformation through coaching sessions and workshops. www.livingwithawe.com; Facebook: Living With AWE: Awareness Wisdom Empowerment.

Jan Schipman is a multi-sensory animal communicator, energy healer, and Reiki Master. Her passion is working with animals to heal their lives and receive their beautiful messages. Through their messages, she and the animals help people tap into their inner selves for healing and strengthening the human-animal bond.

Jani Metzger McCarty: Celebrating Life in her sixties, Jani McCarty offers enthusiastic inspiration, compassionate guidance, and structured support to other Spiritual beings sharing this physical journey. Author, Transformational Teacher & Heal Your Life Coach®, her joy is in living in the present, her relationship with nature, and sharing love from her grateful heart. www.janimccarty.com.

Jean Pomeroy is a Certified Meditation Instructor and the Founder of Workforcemeditations.com and LifeforceMeditations.com. Jean's companies help people live with more peace and ease at the workplace, and at home, through impactful guided meditations. Jean is an inspirational public speaker, and an advocate to help employers reduce workplace stress. www.workforcemeditations.com, www.lifeforcemeditations.com.

Jennifer Ross: After a life-changing experience with Louise Hay Philosophies, I yearned to inspire others to be their own beautiful selves and to create the life of their dreams. Positive and beautiful changes in my life are inspiring. I had a dream and a vision; I chased it and created it! www.heartsoflove.com.au.

Julie Ann Marie is an intuitive soul healer, spiritual teacher, psychic/medium and animal communicator. She guides and supports people on the path of harmony, inner joy, peace and freedom. This heart centered approach brings understanding and deepens your relationship with yourself, other people, animal companions and nature. Website: www.julieannmarie.com.

Julie Gale is a Colorado-based Nature-focused Intuitive Healer. She is studying to achieve a Master's Degree in Transpersonal Psychology, working full-time at a software-services company and creating handmade items to promote healing. Follow her at www.facebook.com/julieannegale/ and www.facebook.com/JoelieFarm/

Julie Geigle is a gifted trance channeler for Metatron, a 4th generation Psychic Medium and Healer. She is the host of "Angel Talk Tuesday" and "Angel Healing Wednesdays." Pick up your free gift "Manifesting Miracles" at www.juliegeigle.com and book your next appointment to gain clarity and direction in your life.

Kallie Johnston: I have always loved writing and took joy in learning how tough the English language can be, but how beautifully it can touch someone within. I appreciate the chance to share some of my thoughts with you in a guided meditation.

Karen Cowperthwaite, founder of Souly Sister is a gifted angel messenger, spiritual counselor and speaker. Her gentle nature supports individuals of all ages to move forward and reconnect to their spirit. She is lovingly nudged by the angels to provide intuitive and heart healing coaching services. Contact:karen@soulysister.com; www.soulysister.com.

Karen J. Lewis is a Psychic, Health Intuitive, and Life Coach, as well as a live radio show host on 12Radio.com's Soul to Sole. You can contact Karen through her website at www.karenjlewis.com

Karen Paolino Correia is an international writer, teacher, and speaker, known for her authenticity and passion. For twenty years, she has helped thousands of people across the globe, through her books, workshops, retreats, certification programs, and private sessions. Karen is the author of five books. Visit Karen's website, www.createheaven.com.

Karen S. Itin: She was raised in Indiana walking the white sandy beaches. She studied Psychology and Interior Design, calls herself an artist and loves books. She and her husband share their home where they enjoy growing a vineyard. She loves spending time with her two sons and dog.

Katherine Glass comes from a lineage of psychic sensitives and healers. Born in the caul (also known as the veil or hood)—long considered a sign of true psychic ability— Katherine has been using her gifts of insight and healing to bring help and healing to others for over 25 years. www.katherineglass.com.

Katina Gillespie Ferrell is a writer, certified workshop facilitator, New Kadampa Tradition practitioner, and employee experience professional. She enjoys adventures with her husband, Charles, volunteering, hiking, dharma, physical fitness, empowering others to shine their Light and sharing time with her family and close friends.

Katrina L. Wright is a consummate~artist, creator and conscious entrepreneur. A lifelong seeker of Truth, yogi, and avid meditator who enjoys living from her 'heart cave', working with kids and inspiring others to greatness. She holds an M.A. In Spiritual Psychology from the University of Santa Monica and resides in Southern California.

Kelli Adkins wears many hats as an RN, coach, author, speaker and podcast Host. She's also a mom and chronic illness warrior. Through her own struggles, Kelli has not only survived, she has thrived! Now her passion is lighting the way for others to do the same. www.EveryDaylivingwithKelli.com.

Kelli Lee Sappenfield is a fifth-generation metaphysician, intuitive, transformational teacher, international speaker, and author. Through her private and group coaching, workshops, and speaking engagements, she has helped people reclaim their true selves—mind, body, and spirit— so they too can live their dreams—without having to die first! www.kellileesappenfield.com.

Kia Abilay is an Akashic Records Teacher, Energy & Intuitive Communicator & One Spirit Interfaith Minister. Kia worked at the Wellness Center at The Omega Institute in Rhinebeck, NY for 13 seasons. Kia is from Hawaii. She has a long distance and in person practice in Uptown Kingston, NY. www.rainbowheart.net.

Kimber Bowers: Through Clinical Hypnotherapy, Reiki, Coaching, Qigong, and her personal line of Flower Essences, Kimber's purpose in this life is to serve as a reflection of the Love that IS, allowing others to discover it within their own realities and within their own souls. www.lovinglighthw.com.

Kris Groth is a craniosacral energy healer, spiritual mentor, intuitive artist and author. She is passionate about helping people connect with their soul and the divine, bringing light and healing to the world. Offering healing/mentoring sessions in-person and phone, and guided sound healing meditations using crystal singing bowls. www.krisgroth.com.

Kyra Schaefer, CHT is the cofounder of the Holistic Speakers Guild. A membership site for authors to get their message to the world through speaking. HSG offers speaker and business training. Here, you can gain more exposure and mastermind with others just like you. www.holisticspeakersguild.com.

Liana Salas is a life and health coach, personal trainer and group fitness instructor. She co-authored *'Living Your Purpose with Sunny Dawn Johnston & Friends'*. Liana has an inspirational weight loss and personal transformation story. She combines her education in psychology, nutrition and fitness to help others transform their lives. www.LianaSalas.com.

Linda Lee is a licensed Heal Your Life workshop leader and coach. She offers workshops throughout Los Angeles and Orange counties in California. Linda spent 25 years as an investigative reporter and editor; her spiritual work has been published by Visionary Insight Press and Science of Mind magazine. lindalee113@verizon.net.

Lindsley Silagi, is an educator and professional coach with a private coaching practice, Step By Step Results!, located in Santa Teresa, New Mexico where she lives happily with her husband, Lon. Lindsley loves dance, art, music, nature, little kids, hot springs, gardening, books, striking up a friendship, photography, and travel.

Lisa A. Clayton is founder of Source Potential, a human development company; serving as master teacher, certified facilitator, intuitive coach, inspirational key-note speaker and spiritual leader helping individuals reclaim their passion, power and potential through whole heart learning. Lisa is an ordained Angel Celebrant and provides individual Angel readings and workshops. www.lisaaclayton.com.

Lisa Eleni Battaglino-Nelson: I am a proud mother of two amazing people, an intuitive artist of many media and an engaged high school English teacher. I have also developed healing workshops that encourage others to find their light, embrace it and let it shine through art, journaling and connecting to others.

Lisa Hardwick is a Writer, Publishing Consultant, Artist, and Certified Workshop Leader. She enjoys traveling with her husband, Ken, spending time with her grandchildren, Maci, Cole, Max and Ava, and going on fun adventures with BFF, Chicago Mermaid.

Lori Kilgour Martin is an Angelic Counselor and Musical Theatre artist from Canada. She is a co-author in *365 Days of Angel Prayers*, and the *365 Book Series.* Trained through AngelsTeach, she feels honored to walk in divine partnership with the angelic realm. Visit Lori at: www.diamondheartangel.com.

Maggie Chula is a Spiritual Teacher, Psychic Channel, a Healer for the Soul. She will help you connect to your source vibration and create a partnership with your soul wisdom. Be encouraged and supported in your journey to create divine health and well-being on every level of life today. www.MaggieChula.com.

Mandy Berlin, M.Ed., is an author, teacher, coach, psychic, speaker, and retired scientist. She authored/co-authored four books, including *Death Is Not "The End"*, based on her mystical and uncanny experiences. Her Joy is in teaching/coaching her Law of Attraction approach and helping others who have sustained grief and loss. www.mandyberlin.com.

Marion Andrews: A lifetime of searching and exploring followed by illness, Marion Andrews discovered her true calling as a Reiki Master, Teacher and Life Coach. Sharing her light and love at the Chrysalis Wellness Center, she helps others emerge from their own cocoon and fly as beautiful butterflies. Discover more at www.marionandrews.com.

Marla Steele became a Professional Pet Psychic in 2001 blending animal communication, energy healing, essences and aromatherapy. Marla creates products and classes to teach others how to love, guide and heal their pets at a deeper soul level. She has been featured on several national radio and TV shows. www.MarlaSteele.com.

Micara Link is an Integrative Therapist, Author, and Love Activist. She blends energy work, intuition, soul coaching®, yoga, somatic experiencing® and mindfulness as a whole-person approach to healing, awakening and empowerment. You can find other free guided meditations on her website at www.MicaraLink.com.

Michelle Beltran is a globally recognized intuitive spiritual teacher. She hosts the iTunes podcast The Intuitive Hour: Awaken Your Inner Voice. She authored the award-winning psychic development book, *Take the Leap: What It Really Means to Be Psychic.* She was featured at Hay House Radio and Hay House World Summit. www.MichelleBeltran.com.

Michelle McDonald Vlastnik: Mystic Intuitive, Inter-dimensional Story Weaver for Soul Remembrance, Angel Abundance Ambassador of Light & Love, Inner Child Advocate, Author, Frequency Holder & Keeper of Light. My movement is the Love vibration, empowerment through becoming our Authentic Self, living on Purpose, and healing Mother Earth. Facebook.com/HighEnergySixSensoryPersonalTraining; www.VibewithMichelle.com.

Misty Proffitt-Thompson is a best-selling author, teacher, speaker, Certified Angel Card Reader, Certified Angelic Life Coach, and Mind, Body, Spirit Practitioner. She helps those who struggle to find their purpose, so they can feel validated and obtain clarity. Misty is married, has four children and four grandchildren. www.mistymthompson.com.

Nancy Newman is a licensed Heal Your Life® coach, registered Master Toe Reader, empath and intuitive with a live call-in radio show, SOUL TO SOLE, on 12Radio. You can contact Nancy for a toe reading or to answer your questions through her website, or 12Listen, where she is an advisor. www.toelady.com; www.12Listen.com; www.12Radio.com.

Neen Forder is an Author and Spiritual Consultant. This mediation was inspired by a channeled message from Neen's Rock Star Angel Steve. You can read more about their story in her latest book *You Make My Heart Sing* (*Life with a Rock Star Angel*) which you can buy from www.rockstarangelbook.com.

Paula Obeid shares her love with the world providing services, education and products that allow individuals to lovingly move through life with joy and ease. Her company www.PUREatHOME.com offers Organic Angelic and Chakra Essential Oil Blends to assist with life especially during meditations. She provides holistic services at www.BLISSALWAYS.com.

Renée Essex-Spurrier is a lightworker, best-selling author and founder of Angelic Creations. She always works from the heart, and with the angelic realms, helps people heal their lives, achieve their dreams, and experience beautiful miracles and synchronicities along the way! For more information, meditations and FREE Oracle Card Readings: www.angelic-creations.net

Rev. Jamie Lynn Thompson's passion is helping to empower and uplift others to let their Sparkle Shine and Live Toadily Divine. She is a Spiritual Ambassador, Faith Healer, Angel Practitioner, Reflexologist, Spiritual Life Coach, and owns Rev. Jamie Lynn's Toadily For You Gifts. Find her on Social Media @RevJamiLynn. www.RevJamieLynn.com.

Robin Lynn Harned is a Reiki Master/Teacher, Hatha Yoga Instructor, Ordained Minister, Certified Mind Body Spirit Practitioner and Administrative Assistant to Sunny Dawn Johnston. Robin offers Chakra Clearing Reiki sessions to her clients with a focus on the 7 Chakras. Contact Robin at robin@sunnydawnjohnston.com.

Rosemary Hurwitz has studied and taught the Enneagram, a holistic system for understanding personality to spirit consciousness for 15 years. She is on faculty at Common Ground, Harper College in Chicago and Univ. of Wisconsin-Milwaukee. For her workshop schedule, private Life coaching sessions for emotional wellness, connect at www.spiritdrivenliving.com.

Sandy Turkington has 35 years of experience as a teacher and demonstrator in disciplines of Angels, Energy work and Mediumship. She is a minister and P.H.D. with degrees in Divinity and Spirituality. She is an author and certified in many other courses as well. www.sandyturkington.com.

Sarah Auger is a spiritual seeker who is always eager to learn and offer love. As a holistic counselor, mantra meditation instructor, Reiki practitioner, and angel-card reader, she dedicates herself in helping others to step into their own power and light. www.sarahmckay.com.

Shalini Saxena Breault: Creator of Swan Goddess LLC and Co-Creator of Sacred Moon Fertility. Also, a Reiki Master/Teacher, Crystal Singing Bowls player, Gong player, Vedic Mantra Chanter/Teacher, Raindrop Therapy/HypnoFertility practitioner and Retreat Leader; Co-Author in the best-selling book, *365 Days of Angel Prayers;* Creates divinely-inspired malas, notecards, bling apparel and workshops/classes. www.swangoddess.com.

Shanda Trofe is independent publisher and author coach specializing in book-writing and marketing strategies for first-time authors, coaches, speakers and entrepreneurs. Through her flagship program, *Publish Like a PRO*, she coaches indie authors through each phase of the book-writing and publishing process, from idea to publication. www.shandatrofe.com.

Skye Angelheart is an experienced Angel Intuitive, Crystal Healer, Holistic Wellness Practitioner, and Reiki expert. Using her knowledge of holistic healing, she customizes sessions for her clients and their cherished animals. Skye is passionate about offering exceptional services that support her clients in rediscovering their authentic hearts. www.skyeangelheart.com.

Sunny Dawn Johnston is a bestselling author, speaker, psychic medium and publisher. She helps people connect with their heart and release what holds them back from being their greatest version of themselves. Combining the unconditional love of a mother and the tell-it-like-it-is honesty of a best friend, Sunny helps people move into a higher vibration of living and Being. www.sunnydawnjohnston.com.

Susan Barrett: I am a writer, Angel Communicator, Certified Prayer Practitioner. I am a former Health Care Administrator. I attended the University of South Florida and currently live in Cave Creek, AZ.

Susan Luth Leahey is a certified coach, working with her clients to support them in identifying their goals and achieving their desires. Her work offers insights and tools, opening new paths to self-awareness, perspectives and ultimately connecting more fully with one's own intuition.

Terri Beaver lives in a small town in southern Nevada, next to Hoover Dam, and Las Vegas. This gave her a small-town attitude with funny quirks that Las Vegas will add to anyone's personality. Terri's greatest joys are her family, God and good friends.

Tina Palmer is an entrepreneur, influencer, and coach. Tina loves to mentor women on their transformation. She does this by helping women shed layers and finding the authentic beautiful woman inside. Tina has created financial freedom by believing in herself, facing her fears, and pushing outside her comfort zone. www.tinapalmer.com.

Tonia Browne is a bestselling author, teacher and coach. Her writing includes coaching strategies, spiritual insights and personal anecdotes. She takes a holistic approach to change. Her book *Spiritual Seas: Diving into Life* shares strategies to help you ride the waves of your own life. Connect with Tonia at toniabrowne.com or www.toniabrowne.com.

Trish Bowie is Married, Mother, Grandmother, Author, Motivational Speaker, Coach, Facilitator. Trish has committed her life to teaching others how to heal themselves. Trish has 21 years' experience as a Reiki Master/Meditation Teacher and is certified in many other modalities and techniques. She offers 24 different workshops and training.

Vicki Snyder-Young is a Professional Psychic Medium, Angel Intuitive, Energy Healer and Coach. She sees clients at her Shop in NY or by phone/skype. With an innate, keen sense of knowing, she can help you realize that you are empowered and destined to live an amazing life. Contact her at vickisnyder138@gmail.com or www.vickisnyder.com.

Wayson Wight: I have been actively practicing mindfulness in many forms for years. This practice has had a profound impact on every aspect of my life. I am a creator. I love nature photography and writing, and the tenants of mindfulness have allowed me to tap deeper into my creative nature. www.waysonwight.com.

Zing Nafzinger is a teacher who uses words, concepts and visualizations to get across metaphysical understandings. She is a healer and artist, crafting her services from her communications with higher realms of vibration. She prepares custom Soul Retreats for experiencing delight within the enchantment that is Provence in southern France. www.SoulRetreatsProvence.com

We Appreciate You!

We hope you have loved the meditations and the beautiful messages of peace, light and healing that these amazing authors have shared within the pages of this book. It is our intention to help you see and feel how powerful beginning your day with meditation can truly be … and the fantastic effect it can have on your life.

In appreciation, we'd like to offer you a FREE audio download of a guided meditation by the author and publisher, Sunny Dawn Johnston. Please go to: https://sunnydawnjohnston.com/michaelguidebook to download your free copy of one of her most popular guided meditations, the *Archangel Michael Meditation.*

Also, won't you be an Angel for us? If you liked the book, please go to Amazon.com and post a review letting others know how much you love it. The more reviews we have, the more visible the book becomes, and the more people begin a meditation practice and start their day off right. Just imagine what the ripple effect of that could be.

Also, make sure you check out our website for new books and new author opportunities at: https://sdjproductions.net/

Finally, if you are into social media, be sure to "Like" our Facebook page at https://www.facebook.com/sunnydawnjohnstonproductions/. Here you will find Facebook Live videos, news and information on current events and products.

We are all so appreciative of your love and support.

Blessings of Love & Light,

Sunny Dawn Johnston & SDJ Productions